The Irrational Journey

Pauline de Rothschild

THE
IRRATIONAL
JOURNEY

Harcourt, Brace & World, Inc., New York

To Diana Vreeland and Glenway Wescott

The Irrational Journey

ONE night in December, a man decided to leave his house and his vineyards, his work of translating Elizabethan poets into French, to spend two months in a country unfamiliar to him. He and his wife would leave for Russia the day after Christmas, and return in March.

They were in the habit of taking long trips together, to Turkey, or Persia, or Denmark, but not to a half-arctic country, in midwinter. They chose winter because of all seasons it is the most Russian. Winter is a season for Russians alone, several renowned captains had noted in passing.

We took all the advice that was offered us and even greater quantities of warm clothing. Just before leaving, we were thoughtfully given a straw picnic basket with an alcohol lamp, not for picnics but to make our tea in our rooms, if needed. We also took a military tin trunk, filled with books.

"What will we do in the evenings?" said Philippe.

"We'll see. There will be theater, or something to read. Or perhaps, with luck, people."

Every traveler feels larger than life. In some countries this makes the visitor seem in the way. Not there, not in Russia.

We squandered time. We returned to the places we liked, saw again and again the people we admired.

There was the sharing of some strange excitement.

3

Leningrad

We arrived in Leningrad late at night. The airport was sound-
less, covered in snow, white, except for low blue lights flickering near the ground. A tall blond young man took us through
customs. They looked at nothing, appeared uninterested. I had
been told that it would seem unflattering to bring no jewelry,
or only imitation, but to take merely what I could wear or carry
in one bag, and, above all, to declare it.

"I have some jewelry," I said, and pulled out a pair of dia-
mond earrings shaped like ribbon bows and a flower made of
diamonds and sapphires. When they were stretched out on the
palm of his hand, the tall young man glanced at them. "Small
diamonds," he said, and handed them back to me, smiling.

We were off. In an old-fashioned limousine with hardly any
luggage space, so we sat bolt upright, in a sort of grotto of suitcases. The streets were still brightly lit. People were walking
about, rather slowly, talking and posturing in the cold. Shopping.
The big stores stay open until ten, the food shops, always very
full, until eleven. Otherwise, said our driver, when would you
do your marketing? When, indeed?

Off to our first winter in Russia. Like children arriving at a new school, we knew nothing, who or what of the faces we would meet in the next two months. And like children in some old-fashioned world, we were immediately put in the hands of our nannies.

The nannies are the Intourist people. They nest downstairs in every large hotel. From afar, when you are asked precisely, oh so precisely, what you wish to see, when and where, you wonder if this particular travel bureau is not a little overinterested in travel, your travel. In reality, the Intourists are a group of excellent governesses. "Full-breasted, agreeable ladies," said Philippe. Not very different from agreeable, full-breasted ladies anywhere, except for their higher heels and their soft, caressing Russian voices. Low, almost grave, these voices have the beat of poems in them, and in the men's an almost feminine tenderness. They are as susceptible to their own voices as we are. Standing on street corners, they talk to each other as if the one wished to enchant the other.

The nannies try to make everything easy for you, treating you like an attractive child who must be protected. From the cold, from lack of knowledge, from a ballet that is not quite perfect.

Like all good nannies, they are firm about time, good manners, and the dates of your comings and goings. They hesitate a little before telling you a thing is possible, which reminds you still further of your childhood. It is only when you wish to change your dates that they develop neurasthenia. For the simple reason that more than one hundred million Russians travel, at all times, filling all planes and most trains, in a country of a baffling size. One central office in Moscow, floating somewhere high above the local offices, takes care of all this. It works, but it is delicate. Changes are discouraged.

We listened. Your guide is your interpreter. You have a car and an interpreter three hours a day. After that, you may keep the interpreter, but to keep the car you will have to pay extra. Here are the tickets for your meals. Almost all restaurants accept these. When you have no more tickets, you will have to pay. (Almost impossible, even with lengthy meals and many guests, to get through the tickets.) Why did you choose to come in the winter? But we love the cold! And where can Philippe get that sort of fur hat, with ear muffs? A *shapka*? Two or three lovely smiles. We are almost Russians.

Bears

Not attractive, the rooms of that first night. Small, with stenciled walls imitating a brocade, a fashion of the turn of the century, not very good to start with. Narrow beds, possessed of the dreariest of printed blankets. The lamps were consoling: tall, winged, Napoleonic gilded ladies, carrying lamp shades. At one time they must have been candelabra in a great house.

The following day, after remarking to the Intourist ladies that we were too large for our rooms—did they not think so too?—we were moved to an apartment, small but superb. Its dark-blue and bright-red drawing room housed, for the purpose of contemplation, twenty-one bronze bears. On dressing tables in the big hotels, a luxury unknown to ours: handsome silver boxes, small silver trays, occasional silver-backed brushes. They are the flotsam and jetsam of pre-1917 traveling cases, the redistributed bureau sets. Each object in the room carries a small metal inventory number, a sort of dog tag, one item of the immense Inventory of the State.

Sleeplessness

All night long, we keep hearing the swish of brooms in the street. It is the old women brushing the snow from the pavements. They work in shifts, bundled in colorless woolens, shaped like gray haystacks.

Before we went to sleep, we observed with interest the first sign of the great Russian cold. Double windows, of course. What was interesting was a strip of paper two inches wide, glued all along the cracks and hinges on the inside of the outer window. A man comes and puts these strips on about October fifteenth. The windows remain sealed till spring. All windows. As you walk along the streets, you see that a few adventurous souls have an occasional pane that can be opened. But it is usually sufficient, to cool or air a room, to open the inner window.

The Tsar's Daughter

It is 9:15. The day is the color of soft brown fur, under a gentle, widely spaced snow. The night lights are still on. They illuminate the broad five-sided square bordered by flesh-colored houses with their flat white pilasters. A snowplow goes by. The ground becomes immediately white again. Light never seems to strike a surface, but appears to come through walls as something latent and luminous. Not unlike Glenway Wescott's description of a woman's beauty: "A skin by which you can see to read," said Glenway. A spotlight hits, high and solitary over a roof, a small square of red cloth of the brightest and lightest red, taut in the wind, beating.

The Tsar's daughter's palace is across the way, built for her at the turn of the century. She refused to live in it because from her windows her father's statue, a huge bronze rider on a still-larger horse, turned its back to her. What was her real reason, do you think?

The Scapegoat

Downstairs, our interpreter was waiting. A strong young woman who enjoyed her good looks, she wore a stiff fur hat straight across her brow. She liked this hat very much and never took it off. We would take our car to the Neva. In the car, there was no question of opening the windows, completely frosted over. This did not disturb our interpreter, who would point out the buildings—St. Isaac's, the Admiralty, the Winter Palace—as we passed, blind and bowing, behind our ice-bound windows.

That day at lunch, for the first time, we heard of the Scapegoat.

Everything in our interpreter's face is round. A round nose, a round mouth, round pink cheeks, and wide-apart brown eyes. She complains a little of her lipstick. Like all Soviet cosmetics, it blurs, and does not last. She and her young husband are buying an apartment. In a stone house, which is more expensive and for which you had to wait longer, but which is nicer. Philippe asked her what they were paying for it. It came to somewhere around three thousand dollars. This seemed a great deal for a young couple.

"My mother in law is helping us," she said. "She inherited some money when my father-in-law died."

"Inherited?"

"Yes. He was good engineer and they were well off. It was only for a while that she was very poor. When he was in a concentration camp. Yes, he was in a concentration camp, and yet he was a militant Communist."

"What happened, then?"

"A denunciation. A denunciation was sufficient in those days. We never knew from whom."

"It was never questioned?"

"Oh no. But that was in Stalin's day." . . .

"Ah, but since Stalin that has changed." . . . "We are no longer . . ." We were to hear this time and time again. When Khrushchev laid bare the bones of his predecessor, he raised a Culprit for all to see. Stalin could be blamed for everything that had gone wrong with the regime. Because the regime runs your daily life, the blame was his for what had gone wrong with your life. All that had been borne in silence, the costs that had been too high to pay but had been paid. They would always be thankful to the garrulous old man for letting so much air into the country. It is healthy, they now said, to recognize what is wrong. The old Fox had died and become the Scapegoat. No amount of rehabilitating will take the spots out of those small hands.

The First Walk

The voluptuousness of having one's eyelashes lengthen with frost and one's furs crinkle a little when one breathes. We walked, first one way, then back, then back again, the better to see, to see.

There is a curious quality about the past in Russia, not the presence, but the immediacy. Peter the Great is here, and Catherine, and Lenin. The War and the Revolution. These people are image-makers at work. They have the conjurer's gift. The Revolution is here, the War is there. Elsa Triolet, the Russian-born French writer, says that they go from the daily to the legendary faster than most.

"So We Gave Him This City"

This is an immaterial city. Suspended, light and quivering over the marshes it has replaced. One forgets that in winter all its canals, all its rivers are white, long white veins, and along this white, the river banks are softened out so that there is no difference between earth and water. Along them the broad flanks of its houses: moss green, buff, and the color cream-with-coffee-in-it that Théophile Gautier called *ventre-de-biche.* Then more furry greens, one apricot color, then the rectangular red walls of four houses, and a low palace, red.

But this is nothing. This is only what the eye breaks against on the ground. There is another city above this one, weightless, spired, and domed, divided from the other by mists. Across the river, over the fortress of Peter and Paul, a long golden needle, slim and still, floats alone, disembodied.

When Peter the Great wished his new city to grow, he passed a law. No one in all the Russias could build except in St. Petersburg. The houses must be of stone, then painted. Because of fires a second law imposed wide spaces between the houses. So that you get along the river an alternate pattern of wall and air, a checkerboard of color and snow.

Philippe said to our interpreter: "Peter the Great imagined this city, created it, pulled it out of the marshes. It was called St. Petersburg. Then, Petrograd. He had earned this. Why did you change its name to Leningrad?"

"When Lenin died, we wanted to give him the very best we had. So we gave him this city."

Advantages and disadvantages of the sheltered life. No foreign newspapers, except two Communist dailies, one in English, and the other the French *L'Humanité*. No foreign-language weeklies, except one. This is prepared in Moscow for some preconditioned foreigners and is of an unbelievably low intellectual standard, written in Prince Igor English.

No telephone books. There are none printed.

There is no way of ringing anyone up if you haven't the number.

Letters reached one from the U.S. in about three weeks. For customary visitors to Russia, letters from Paris take about eight days. These delays are slightly illogical, since there seems to be no censorship on cables, and you can telephone anywhere in the world—within a quarter of an hour if you are in Moscow, and if you are away from Moscow, within the hour—for as long as you wish the conversation to last.

In Certain Public Libraries

There is one Russian weekly that carries foreign dispatches, articles, and reappraisals or analyses of the news by various foreign newspaper writers. These are reprinted without change, and without comment. This weekly is available only in certain public libraries, and can be consulted there.

The Admiralty

At a right angle with the river, the Admiralty's bright-yellow walls, broken at regular intervals by white columns. They stretch along the Neva, along the public square. There is a double repetition of white, at the lower level the frozen trees, and above, the white columns against the yellow walls. Topping this, the sun on some gilded shape. Farther along, a pale young green, the Winter Palace.

Windows on the Neva

At the Hermitage, we presented our credentials to Madame E.: a sort of bridge of tact and warmth between the invisible directors of the museum and the outside world.

Her office had enormously high windows giving on the Neva, and the usual Russian desks, most comforting, because they seemed big enough to lie down on. We would meet there twice a day. We would have conversations, very worldly in the sense of light and teasing questions and answers that did not take you very far afield. She said that she would have liked to invite us for lunch on New Year's Day, but that couldn't be, and she offered us some delicious chocolates disguised as large gold coins. She planned our life in the Hermitage, what we would see, whom we would meet. There began a series of relationships, with other museum officials, curators, authorities, more bewitching even than the works of art.

The Meteor

There was, for instance, the Meteor.

She was the head of the Byzantine department, a world-renowned scholar, and we had been most anxious to see her. No appointments had been feasible. She came upon us one day in a long gallery. "I am a meteor," she said, and vanished. Eventually she gave us a long afternoon's care, way past closing time, and, as a proper meteor, she would turn to light up dark rooms and dim cases. We told her that we knew less than nothing about Byzantine art, and instead of boring her this seemed to refresh her spirits. After this, when we were with other curators in a different part of the museum, she would suddenly appear for a few seconds' conversation. There was something long and English about the shape of her face, and she combined languor with speed as the English so often do.

The Rich People

Then, there was the passing glimpse of the Rich People. We were with Madame E., curator of modern French painting, whose gay voice and witty looks had brought her three husbands. The last one, a brilliantly intelligent Armenian, had been the director of the Hermitage. "Very intelligent. But what a temper! Impossible in the house, that temper," she said. She would then touch the gray lamb of her small fur cuffs and collar and walk faster, swinging the pleats of her gray tweed skirt. Perhaps one should love some husbands for show, others for use.

We passed a Bonnard.

"This landscape was given to us by a collector," she said. "Two years ago."

"People here still have collections?" asked Philippe.

"Why not? Of course," sounded the happy voice. "We have everything here, even Rich People."

"And they have collections?"

"Of course." With an undertone, rather offended, of: Do you think capitalists the only ones to have collections?

We pondered this later. "What exactly does it mean?" said Philippe.

"Mean? I don't know, I haven't seen any rich people as yet. I do know that if someone came up to me and said, 'There goes a rich man,' it wouldn't mean much because 'rich' is a general term and still as vague to me as to many other people. But with you, it is different. You are supposed to know what a rich man is. So that if someone says to you, 'That man is rich,' it must be so. No one comes up to me and says, 'This horse is a good horse.' Whatever for?"

Slander

The inn at Tsarskoye Selo (the Tsar's village, now called Pushkin) is a simple, square, three-storied wooden building, painted white, rather like the Massachusetts houses of the early nineteenth century. The room in which we sat for lunch was light, high, rather like a schoolroom. Through its long windows and the interlacing of the furry white branches of the frozen trees, the domes of Catherine's chapel could be counted. Freshly gilded in the sun against a Mary-mother-of-God blue sky. Five, seven onion domes, sometimes nine, never anywhere an even number.

Madame N. is a great beauty. In the tradition of those who charm the beasts off the trees and any other wanderers of the animal kingdom. She has large gray-green eyes, straight black lashes, dark hair brought back into a knot, pearl earrings through her pierced ears. She wore soft cardigans of the type we all own, buttoned up to the neck. When she walked or stood she kept her arms close to her ribs, which increased her length and narrowness. A tweed skirt. A small jewel. Nothing, yet *le comble de l'élégance,* as the French say. Which is wrongly translated, I think, as the "height of elegance." It is more: "elegance fulfilled."

All Russians have patriotic principles. Madame N.'s came out rather unexpectedly. A Frenchwoman, across the table, spoke of Catherine the Great somewhat wistfully. How well the Empress had organized herself, reigning, collecting, taking her pick of any men at court, *"se tapant,"* the equivalent of helping oneself a little too quickly and recklessly but with thorough enjoyment, *"se tapant les ambassadeurs."* "No, I've never heard that about Catherine the Great," came the prompt reply. "She never slept with foreigners."

Greens

One is struck by the number of green-colored houses. Everything Rastrelli, Catherine's architect, built is blue-green or green, so, of course, the Winter Palace, which was returned to its original green after 1917. The inventor of Boeuf Stroganoff lived in a charming green eighteenth-century palace on a wide canal. The café called the Frogs, where one goes to eat ices, is green. On the other hand, the nineteenth century is mostly yellow and white, like the Yussupoff house from which Rasputin was dragged, a very large man to die in so small a river.

At Tsarskoye Selo, Catherine's head gardener lived next to the palace in a large house of the most exquisite proportions, the color of a heart of artichoke, and corresponded there with Jefferson.

Just to look at this house is a form of happiness.

October 24

"On the 24th of October, 1917," reads the sign, "this palace was opened to the People."

It is curious how the Soviets manage to convince the crowds that all that they see belongs to them: I have never felt this to be true elsewhere in any other national collections. Perhaps if the Metropolitan Museum of Art put up a small sign saying, "In 1958 this museum was opened to the People," it would have an agreeable effect.

Silver Tureens

At times, curators of other departments would join us at the Hermitage, and, since they were all friends, would make comments. This was a sort of refresher course for them, and turned our visit into a trip through strangeness, with people getting on and off the bus. There was the morning when the head of the Decorative Arts was to shepherd us. The decorative arts were to include silver, porcelain, glass, such apartments as the Tsarina's, and furniture too perhaps, though I was never to find out. This very tall and imposing gentleman showed us the Sèvres a certain tsar had ordered, the silver tureens Count Orlov, the first lover to show splendor, had brought back from his visit to Paris. Philippe showed no signs of excitement.

Once or twice he would ask, "Isn't Madame N. joining us?"

We passed the great silver service made by Louis XV's silversmith, Germain. Perhaps Philippe was indifferent, I thought, because the silver was black. (Russian museums never clean their silver.)

Philippe turned to the serious and by then somewhat silent man. "I am not interested in Germain," said Philippe.

The serious man quickly stepped to a telephone and dialed a number. "Monsieur de Rothschild only wants to look at Madame N.," he said. "So would you please ask her to come down."

The Seekers

Travelers plunge into the Hermitage the way they would embark on a long sea voyage. Half afloat, half submerged, under waves of objects incased in glass, they go, past doors, past halls, past rooms.

What fetishisms send all of us out like armies, trudging through museums, paying our entrance to them in every corner of the earth we reach?

The man leaning against the glass case is not a bewitched seeker. He is just a man, who has been told that in a world of which he can ask anything, there is no immortality. The promise once made to men, of an afterlife, has largely been taken away. Except for the few, and their beliefs may not be his. But behind him, time lies open. He is here in this museum to see the work of men who went beyond their needs. What has survived may well be life everlasting. Through the glass, he is looking not at a Leonardo, or at an earthen cup, but at some mysterious virtue that will reward him, somewhere, at some other time, perhaps.

In the Middle Ages, people sought for plants with curative

qualities. The Greek herb moly went further, and gave you back your life.

Furs in the Street

The street is a street of bankers. The men are all in fur hats, handsome fur collars on their overcoats; the most modest driver or delivery man has the most perfect astrakhan. They wear their fur *shapkas* with the ear covers not tied down, but standing out. This makes them look like dogs on their hind legs, their fine ears flapping. When the high dogs with the flapping ears go home, the streets seem still more brightly lit.

What makes one turn one's head is the courtesy of the Russians, one to the other. Relationships are gentle. This is a holiday time, and people stop to congratulate each other. The men kiss the women's hands. I don't know if this is just the festive days, or customary.

Under their warmth, a sort of compassion.

Tea and Lessons

The routine of the happy days began to take shape.

The Hermitage would close. Every evening there would be theater, but first tea and my Russian lesson. We would walk home through the square, under the trees, each branch two or three times its size with a shagginess of iced snow standing up on it like hair on end.

Tea came with a sea of strawberry jam. There is a discussion, in Tolstoy, I think, on how to make jam. Liquid, hardly cooked, in the Russian manner, or the German–Western-European way, more long lasting. In our jam the strawberries were left whole, as if you had just picked them and left them about for an hour. The hot toast would be brought. Crushed with their own weight, the berries had the sweet sleepy smell of the fields about them.

My teacher was a university professor, the mother of a small girl of six. She could easily have played Joan of Arc in Anouilh's *L'Alouette*, and she would give us brilliant foreshortened accounts of the play we would be seeing that night, whole sentences made recognizable at key points. She had a straightforward beauty and dignity. Philippe would watch her from under his eyelids, not knowing quite what to make of such good looks and such timidity, without any self-consciousness whatever. Yet with banners flying somewhere.

She would draw outlines for me, of the throat and the palate, in red ink, to get me to place sounds where no sounds had come from before. As a reward, I would be allowed to translate, oh how badly, a Tolstoy fable for children. What I preferred was her talking about her husband and child, suddenly, very quietly, as if these wonderful creatures were in the next room. When we left Leningrad she gave me one of my favorite presents: a recording of Tchekhov spoken by his actress-wife.

Like a Flower

The word "Revolution" is worn like a flower in the buttonhole. People speak of the Revolution the way medieval poets speak of the Spring. The Revolution is a sort of nationality, a country of the mind, their success and their strength.

In the back of our minds, however, remains the thought that

there is something of Lucifer in the Revolution, and that the revolutionaries are the Fallen Angels. Something very faint, an astonishment once-removed, comes over us when the Fallen Angels are sitting down at table, successful, happy, laughing.

The Fallen Angels, bright and cheerful at home, meet with strange reactions in other countries.

Two women curators of the Hermitage were in Paris. They found that if they said they were Russians, they would be taken for White Russians. This they did not want. "Of course we are *not*," they explained, "and when the nice man staying at the same hotel said to us in the elevator, 'What are you?' we answered, 'U.S.S.R. We are Soviet citizens.' The man leaned against the wall of the small elevator and loosened his tie."

Books

We had brought our books, what we thought necessary for traveling. In truth, a library. Herodotus, very useful, with his Scythian-Russians of the fifth century B.C. Théophile Gautier's *Voyage en Russie*, in the winter of 1865. Maurice Baring up to 1912. Some recent writers, including Constantin Paustovsky and Victor Shklovsky (his marvelous *Letters That Do Not Speak of Love*). No books on the Revolution, no information on the present day. The surprise comes late at night, reading on the spot, in the flesh, so to speak, the great Russians: the aristocrat Tolstoy's novels *Anna Karenina* and *Resurrection* become social tracts; the cosmopolitan Turgenev writes with controlled despair; the Revolution is present in each line of the self-taught Gorki; Tchekhov the doctor asks for a more hopeful tomorrow. Dissimilar talents, dissimilar stations of life, and everywhere the same roar and the same lament. There seemed to be no way out of this sickness, this waste. Lenin's book was entitled *What to Do?** Except for a handful too rich, or too powerful, or too stupid, every class wished for a change, could not get it, and knew the Revolution to be inevitable. Now that the pain has gone, it resembles a fresh beginning, a Spring. Not a resurrection, but a coming to life.

The Hospital

At quarter to five in the morning Philippe came into my room. I had been having one of those delicious nights of insomnia, when if you put out the light for a minute or two, you know that you will not sleep, and can hardly wait to go on with your reading. Philippe stood in the doorway and said, "What are you doing? I have been in pain since two o'clock. I don't know what's the matter with me. I have never had this pain before." His face was gray and he moaned a little. He went back to his room. The hotel was half dark. The night watchman almost asleep. Anyway, whom would one call? Better to wait. Until nine o'clock when the Intourist desk would open.

I would walk from Philippe's room back to mine, listening to the silence and then again the spasms of cries. During the intervals when he was not suffering, Philippe would say, "I have come to Russia to die."

The doctor arrived at ten. I opened the door. Three people stood in front of me, all dressed in white operating gowns and caps. One woman, who was the doctor, and two huge young men, who turned out to be interns. I said rather loudly, so Philippe would not be frightened, "Must you be so many? Could you not come in one at a time?" No.

* Also translated as *What's to Be Done?* The Russian *Chto Delat* is shorter and stronger.

They seemed to have brought a great deal of material in tin suitcases. One of the interns had studied in Holland and was disappointed that I did not speak Dutch. In the meantime, two calls I had placed earlier came in from Paris, one from Philippe's doctor, one from his surgeon. (He had been operated on six months before.) The three diagnoses coincided. The Russian doctor gave him an injection and then insisted he would be better taken care of in the hospital. Philippe acquiesced. Off we went.

In the ambulance, sitting up, he felt the pain come on again, grabbed and held tightly to the hand of the dark young intern. The young man took his hand and patted it seriously and gently as he would his own child's. In the hospital, there was no waiting, and in no time Philippe was sitting up in bed surrounded by three lady doctors, all very large, and all stroking his bare stomach. He seemed enchanted. He soon went to sleep. One of the shots they had given him was to help dissolve the stone in the kidney, I believe they said, and he could go home in a few hours.

I stayed in the hospital watching the new arrivals.

A boy of about fifteen was brought in. He had been hit by a car, and was unwounded, but white, suffering from shock. He was given the same warm care, and tenderly covered. Philippe was not allowed to pay for his X rays or medicines. For the lady doctors the boy's father before going away had left two packages of cigarettes and some matches.

The next day I returned to thank them and to bring some tokens of appreciation. (In this case, small packages of pairs of nylon stockings.) My lady doctors were out. It was their day off. I was taken to see the head doctor and two others, all women, very large and kind. We sat down with my interpreter for the usual exchange of small talk. I remarked that what impressed me most during this whole affair was just that—the extraordinary kindness. The head nurse straightened herself behind her desk and said, "Everywhere in the U.S.S.R. you will meet with kindness." The conversation seemed to have taken on weight. Not dazzling, as Lady Murasaki once sternly remarked at a court function in eleventh-century Japan, where too the light touch had vanished. The woman facing me was probably an old-style enthusiast, a breed almost extinct, or at least unfashionable in today's secure system.

I bowed, hand on the heart, and left.

The heart is much to the fore. One constantly puts one's hand on one's heart, sometimes both hands, especially women. Lucid thought is not to be trusted as much as this heart's instinct, this quickness.

Balloons

When you see a queue you may be quite sure that it is in front of either a tobacco shop or a bookstore. The line-up in front of bookstores before the morning or afternoon opening is startling. Women with white blouses over their heavy winter clothes, enormous as balloons, stand on street corners behind hampers filled with the latest edition of a new book, and sell it as they would oranges, and just as fast.

Though the longest queue in Leningrad is in front of a pastry shop in the Nevsky Prospekt, with the best cakes in all Russia. If anyone is traveling home, or has a birthday, or a small feast, one brings a pastry from this famous shop.

People say, yes, but Rastrelli, an Italian, built the Winter Palace. Charles Cameron, a Scotsman (and what a Scot—with a great classical education and a taste for flowers in decoration made so fresh in their varieties that they would ravish a botanist), built Pavlosk. In short, foreign architects. But how long do they remain foreign? One should remember how one's eye changes in another country with a different weight of light and sky, and certainly a patron of a different weight. With a different length purse strings.

Ledoux, the most hallucinatory of French architects, worked in France from 1762 to 1806, a huge span of time. He exercised, through his pupils and emulators, the greatest influence in Russia of any neoclassicist. He was an offspring of Mycenae wandering around with visions of science fiction in his eyes. He found his proportions in the Temple of Poseidon in Paestum, and in both Palladio and Piranesi, but he wished for other shapes based on the rotations of the planets, cities with elliptical centers fanning out like sunrays. This early Buckminster Fuller designed an agricultural exchange consisting of a round orb like the iris of the eye, in which the door was the pupil, with arched steps leading up to it. The iris was an obsession with him. He had presented his plan for the Besançon theater as a reflection in an eye, the shadings from the iris to the pupil deepening as one neared the focal point of interest.

Columns, Architects, and a Dancer

Ledoux's Russian emulators followed the less adventurous lessons of the master, but their work kept his strength, his versatility and clarity. Certain parts of Leningrad are like taking a

rising fan-shaped. The bases of the windows are like fragments of pale rock. The color of this temple is green, the green of an olive tree. The Neva below is a darker green, with white drifts of snow and ice.

A wide, squat, muscular building. Ledoux would have approved.

Matisse

By now the Matisse rooms in the Hermitage are so famous that one might keep quiet about them. If one could. You go up quite a long way to the top floor, then find two large gray rooms with low ceilings, and there they are, a wild number of Matisses. What are these colors, this incredible freshness? There is something of the early morning of creation still on them. You are given these colors so that you will be present at a feast. The picture was worked out and suddenly the feast was on. The feast of painting. You must see and you must take part. You begin to understand how God felt when he first saw a green field.

There go the young, leaving the Hermitage at dusk, ten, twenty boys and girls in their gray flannel suits, with their bright scarlet scarves tied in a Byronic knot around their necks, the two ends flickering like their eyes.

In this light, as they run one to the other, the eyes are streaks of gray. The faces have the look of young Russian skins in winter, a pale smoothness, which is the unexpected result of the cold together with hothouse temperatures. The women's hands, for instance, are never red.

The Skeptic and His Beliefs

The Skeptic was a writer, a Leningrad acquaintance, who was also a Sage. He unwittingly gave us a view of ourselves which is universal in the U.S.S.R. This view disturbs them more than it does us.

The Skeptic was very short and round and strong, the shape of St. Thomas probably, the sort of bald man who seems to have refused hair at birth. He had firm, mocking views about everything. Except women. With them he was an instant success, probably because they could charm him almost at will. So he had snared with the greatest of ease three or perhaps four beautiful wives. His great love, like Berenson's, was Italian painting. He had traveled much, often to Italy, to conferences of art historians, and to many other countries where research was done, where ideas were being exchanged. I mention the last to show you that he was not an insular but a traveled man.

One evening, very much later, after our return from Moscow, I found myself, because of the warmth, the general happiness, the green-yellow Georgian wine, saying to him, as an American, what a terrifying waste this is, our two countries still almost sealed off from one another, when no two people's qualities on this earth were more an extension of each other's. Why should we not know their use of the heart, their elegance of mind, the gentle, rapid sensitivity of their understanding, the vitality of their love of people, just people? They shared with us an extraordinary sense of tomorrow. We were perhaps more generous than they, our machine was less cumbersome in letting talent and intelligence come to the surface, and, having had no spectacular prophets, we knew more about what made the modern world tick. Wasn't there a formula of some sort, political or economic, that would make a bridge between their world and ours over which we could both safely pass?

"Oh," he answered, "no formula. Above all, no formula. Let

us slip, when possible, between difficulties. But no formula. You see, my dear, if you were to say, for instance, that there is a great deal of liberty here, I would have to say, no, that is not so. On the other hand, if you were to say that you did not exploit the workers, I would have to say that that is not so, either."

There seems to be no question in their minds: what we have, we acquired not by our own efforts but by depriving someone of his rights. We are the exploiters. They see with their own eyes our immense wealth, and our indifference. They think that our promises are not serious. They would agree to our being all very rich, or all moderately poor.

They cannot understand how we can allow misery to be the lot of the incapable, the ungifted, the dumb.

We were given our chance to make the world very much better and missed.

However, this moral distaste and somewhat self-righteous attitude on their part are quickly replaced by the joyful act of presence, of somewhere, somehow, being alive together.

So the men of good will and the evildoers (ourselves) went arm in arm down the street, to see whether the Caucasian bistro was still open.

The Divided Window

The streets around the Hotel Astoria once made up the elegant quarter of Leningrad. The most serene and beautiful townhouses to be seen anywhere outside of London. "A Russian apartment holds the combined resources of English and French civilizations," said a traveler in the seventies. The long windows were made to reflect the selective life, to be looked through on to glistening objects, into the sudden opening of mirrors. Tonight, the rectangle of a dusty pane shows a single light bulb hanging from a long string. A window is divided in two, one half lit, the other dark, visibly halved when two rooms were made out of one. Between the double window, a few pots of flowers, a bottle, a cardboard box of something that must be kept cool. One remembers Anna Karenina entering the house to go upstairs to a ball, so mysteriously dark within the gleam.

1865

Théophile Gautier's *Voyage en Russie* in 1865 was about a winter trip such as ours. "Flowers, a true Russian luxury," he exclaims and in describing them shows us the apartments: "houses burst with them . . . in the hall, up the stair. Magnolia and camellia trees flowering near the gilded ceiling, orchids fluttering around crystal or porcelain lamps, cornucopias of exotic flowers. As in a hothouse. Every apartment is a hothouse." He tells us of a hostess distributing the little bunches of violets that surround a dish of sweets, then going to sit with a few of her guests in a corner of the drawing room, slightly screened from the rest by a trellis of climbers and flowering bean trees. These screens were well tended and kept green and flowering in many rooms. There is a water color of a large bathroom, two trellises halfway between the bathtub and the dressing table.

Today, you see glass kiosks, shaped like small hothouses, as seen through a jeweler's eye. They are filled with jars holding white cornucopias of paper. Inside the cornucopias are paper flowers.

Perhaps, yes, if you grow them in a room, otherwise there are no fresh flowers to be had in the winter in all of Russia. They've had other cats to whip, as the French say.

Elegance. The most fleeting, untractable of qualities. It can be increased, but rarely bought outright.

True elegance is something swift in one's step, some readiness in the turn of the head, something given at once or lightly withheld. Something beyond disappointment.

Yet it is of a strange sort. It does not necessarily show in photographs. Except for the picture in *Time* of Mr. Kosygin, with his daughter, in a gondola in Venice in winter. No visitors ever looked more elegant in a photograph. They are seated, in the back of the black boat, he in a well-tailored town overcoat, black Homburg, one bare hand holding a gloved one. She, bareheaded, gathers at her throat, tight against the Venetian wind, the folds of a soft mink coat. The look on her father's face is one of patient surprise. He seems extremely interested in the fact that this, whatever he is looking at, may not interest him at all.

In the magazines or newspapers the shapes of a few faces give some clue to this elegance, but very little else. Is it, then, the voices, or the fact that they never shove or push, and are not rough-gestured?

It is more some inner, unconscious grace.

Moscow

Red

We are taking the Leningrad-Moscow night train, a favorite of Russians of both cities. Philippe's sleeping hours and mine differ so much that we have luxuriously reserved two sleepers. But the true luxury lies elsewhere: in the double sleepers, each one a room, a red living room, long and very broad, owing to the width of Russian trains. In our solitary smaller sleepers, we had the brilliant reds of the blankets, the brighter carpet, the lamps with their opaline lamp shades, the curtains, and the deep armchair of red facing the bed across a wide table.

Through the glass of the train window in the dark of 8:00 A.M., a white face, a smile, black hair turned up like a Dutch cap, and brilliant penciled eyes: our interpreter, hugging to herself her nylon-fur coat of a Dior shape. We had remarked wistfully to some friends in Leningrad that our guide-interpreters seemed to have the thinnest possible veneer of historical information. This one, the charming Margot, was a computer expert graduating in electrical sciences, and when she lacked information she quickly found a probability that would do until the next time she met us. Complete and serious with knowledge. She had just guided, on a very long trip, fifteen southern Frenchmen who kept repeating, *"Ah, ce n'est pas comme ça à Marseille."* We came to take her light teasing as something that was due us, like a walk or lunch.

The Ornamental Man

She was very much in love with her husband, a ballet dancer. When he was not in performance at the Bolshoi, he would religiously exercise, or "take a class."

"What does he do when he is not dancing?"

"He sleeps."

This strong and good-looking young man evidently needed great restoring drafts of sleep. Did the divisions of his day consist of dancing, listening to her chatter, and sleeping? Yes. This view of the ornamental man is not unusual, and is shared by many Russian women. The men are decorative, lovable, work as little as possible, love to sleep. It is they who have the visions. Meanwhile the women work ceaselessly and form the huge pool of labor, make and hold together by their intelligence and their strength the whole fabric of Russian life. As a natural result, with few exceptions, the top jobs go to the men.

The National

At the Hotel National, the maid, an elderly and exuberant crone, took me into the bathroom, ran her hand over the tub, and showed me her palm with pleasure. Yes, very clean.

The Shape in the Bed

Russian servants do not differ from any other servants except by the amount of what they leave undone. Once you accept the fact that it is boring to give the same service every day, and, worse still, to the same people, relationships are most pleasant, even affectionate.

A friend fretted at finding the outline of her last night's body in the present evening's bed. The remedy is to murmur to those marvelous nannies, the Intourist, could they tell the maid to look a little more closely at the bed. If you are tolerant and, if possible, amused by the maid's eccentricities, everything is righted at once. If you complain and look disapproving, things mysteriously get worse.

Butterfly Wings

The apartment at the National is enormous, shaped like a swallow, with the bedrooms at each end, and the drawing room in the middle. It was filled with Biedermeier, blond-wood and ebony furniture. If Agamemnon had wished to furnish Argos in Biedermeier, this is what he would have ordered. In Philippe's room there was a mirror, low and six feet lengthwise on the wall, in a frame of porcelain flowers the width of an herbaceous border. On a pedestal in the living room, a vase with the effigies of the deceased Emperor and Empress, below this, a concert-size piano, and over our heads a painted ceiling of naked ladies, singularly proper, with butterfly wings. I would sit to read or write far away in the recess of one of the windows, facing in the distance the flowering mirror in Philippe's room, so that returning indoors from the cold and snow seemed somehow connected with this mirror.

It would be nice to teach children from an atlas made up of personal geographies—the shape the South had for Faulkner, Paris as seen by the Atlantic City beauty queen, and, for future generals, maps of unequal importance. What shape had Persia for Alexander? That of a spine perhaps. Or, at the end of a long year, only that of a palace with a room of polished dark stone, his dressing room, where he could see on every wall his reflection. Then there was the death of a friend and a fire. When Hephaestion died, Alexander's grief was so great that you can still hear its distress in the voice of the writer who tells it. He stretched himself out on the body of his friend, and would not leave its side for three days. Later, there was a fire and the great beams of the palace in Persepolis caved in. Evidently the memory of places changes into events.

Moscow had for us the shape of three fortresses: first, the Kremlin; second, the Hotel National and the wide streets surrounding it; and third, the Hotel Metropole, nicely old-fashioned in a skein of ugly streets.

The Breakfast Table

We pulled the breakfast table to face the Kremlin wall, painted a bright buttercup-yellow, with, above it, one small golden cupola.

We were to spend a good deal of time at this table. The Spaniards used to be thought slow. "Let my death come from Spain, for then it will be long in coming." Let my breakfast not come from Russia, O Lord, for I risk having to wait too long. Anywhere from twenty-five minutes to an hour. In the elevators this was the sole subject of conversation among visitors, especially the English.

The Straight Wall

From the door of St. Basil's multicolored cathedral, down the hill of the Kremlin, a wide space of snow leads almost directly into the hall of our Hotel National. The Kremlin wall, yellow outside, straightens behind Lenin's tomb and is of uncovered brick in that part, a straight red curtain along the Red Square. Lesser figures—patriots, generals, Stalin—are buried against this curtain, under small slabs.

Traveling Can Come to an End

We had waited until the light changed around four o'clock to walk into the Kremlin proper, unaware that it was not one building but several, grouped around an inner square: a surprising Venetian palace of faceted stone built by Venetian architects in the fourteen-hundreds, a modern glass theater, a bell tower, the Great Palace, three cathedrals. White heights and golden domes. Traveling had come to some sort of full stop. One had gone long and far. To Turkey for the liquid dark-green inside of a mosque at Brussa. Farther on there had been some bright-pink flat-petaled roses picked up on the brick ground of a market place in Persia, sold for scent. There had been long walks in mists uncertain over some canals. Where doesn't one wander, under the heavy gray roofs in Japan, along the shadow of a wall in Rome? Yet the world perhaps has no greater beauty than this, this cup of white and gold, lined with snow. Is it the white walls and the domes that glisten, or the air, or the gold crosses with their chains? Impossible to tell.

The Map

Our map had other islands: Tolstoy's house, the Bolshoi theater, the outdoor heated swimming pool with the steam rising in the cold and hiding the swimmers except for a sudden bright-red arm. Philippe wished to try this pool, but, happily, we had no bathing suits. Convents and smaller theaters in the periphery. The old Naryshkin palace like a house in children's books, the color of a bright orange, housing a collection of eighteenth-century peasants' and merchants' furniture, painted in clear clashing pinks, yellows, and blues, with flowery tracings of black or green. Along the river in another quarter, the apartment house where Lili Brik, the woman so loved by the poet Mayakovski, lives with her husband, Vasili Katanyan.

In this small apartment we spent our happiest hours.

The Lord

I don't know whether to begin with Lili Brik, who always touched or created legends, and her husband and the people around them, or with our relationship with the Russian Church. In the atheistic Russian world, with its sharp sense of hierarchy, perhaps the Lord should come first. Our religious relationships were intricate and involving. They led to our traveling with deacons, to our lunching in convents with archimandrites and with professors of theology at priests' training centers. I am afraid that this spectacular world was opened by a slight mis-understanding.

The 1905 Baedeker

One morning, Philippe was downstairs receiving a visitor. The tall visitor had a thin, sun-tanned, witty face. He was one of the men who run Intourist. His office was next door, and he had come to see Philippe as some sort of pleasant gesture. When I joined them, he and Philippe had been friends for a long time. The suddenness and completeness of friendships in Russia must be a cause for eternal rejoicing. The visitor asked me if I was enjoying myself and if there was anything in particular I wanted to see. That I was enjoying myself was quite obvious, so I opened a 1905 Baedeker that Liliane de R. had lent me and showed him the names of some eighty churches I wished to see. (Churches may or may not vanish, but in crisscrossing a city to search for them, one discovers its inner, folded-in streets and secret squares.) The charming man looked carefully at the list and pointed out that two revolutions, quite a few fires, a civil war, two world wars had gone by since 1905. I said we would particularly like to see the churches that were function-ing and attend some services. He was silent for a moment. Was he faced with the problem of a very religious woman? As an atheist, he knew none of the veiled questions that would have revealed this condition. On thinking it over, he decided to put us in the hands of the Church, to arrange an appointment with a member of the priesthood, and to accompany us himself to the Metropolite's headquarters with our interpreter. He may have chosen to do this because it was fun and new to him, or because he had never been involved so closely with the religious life.

The interview took place two days later in a building resembling Cardinal Spellman's residence. We were formally ushered in by two butlers and offered morning tea, brandy, caviar, fruit. The Moscow Patriarch, the head of all the churches, was traveling. We were to be received by his representative. Several popes and deacons were introduced, and we sat around a green baize table. Philippe was given a more important high-backed chair, like a sage. This he politely pretended not to notice. Most of them wore gold crosses the length of one's hand, inlaid with aquamarines or amethysts.

The Church's interpreter and ours alternated. It was quite obvious that aside from knowing Philippe's name, the Archimandrite had no idea why we had been brought to see him. Was Philippe a representative of the French government? Or of Israel? Or of some petrol or banking interest interested in convents? He settled finally for the representative of France and voiced many forebodings on de Gaulle's friendly attitude toward Germany. Philippe was evasive, balked at some of the foreign-policy hurdles, and finally murmured that he was interested only in things of the spirit. (Especially since the conversation seemed directed less to him than to our friend of the Intourist, utterly silent.) The talk veered to the numerous foreign travels of the Russian churchmen and the councils they attended. We enumerated the monasteries we hoped to visit.

The Archimandrite suggested we be given a deacon to travel with us, and chose Father Nicolas. Father Nicolas knew every church in Moscow and could also accompany us on our travels. Zagorsk was near, but Vladimir and Suzdal, sacred cities, were far away. Father Nicolas would have faraway churches, closed in the winter, opened, and get in touch with the clergy.

Father Nicolas was young, tall, with a huge body, a pink face, and a russet mustache, and the narrowest and smallest eyes, which seemed somehow to protect him.

During the days that followed we would lose Father Nicolas, and if we worried, our interpreter, a staunch unbeliever, would say, "He is praying to the god." This enlarged our view of Father Nicolas' fervor but somehow diminished the god, no longer God.

Philippe asked what made the Church so rich. The sale of wax tapers, he was told.

Money

It is interesting to be among people who for fifty years, two and a half generations, have had no thought, or, rather, have not been able to think, of money. You were given your due, this was decided somewhere, you had no appeal. You might heap up honors and rewards, but money as a form of prestige and power was useless. Today, people usually have more cash than is needed for what there is to buy. Tickets to the New Year's Eve Gala at the Astoria were selling on the black market, among Russians, for a hundred dollars apiece. The pushing and jostling of a competitive society becomes unnecessary, beside the point.

The lack of a struggle for money is a privilege in itself, and was in England the very basis of the aristocratic mind and upbringing.

We were constantly told that there is a tremendous surge toward a better material life, more comfort, greater ease, and the charms of choice. They would not show this to visiting foreigners.

The Russians' evolution may be like Giacometti's. One evening at the Berniers' he said: "When I was young I didn't want to have money so as to be free of it. Now I like to have money to be free of it."

He wore a gold metal star dangling from a red ribbon. Almost tall, muscular, the usual athlete in a business suit, except for the gold star. The eyes, brooding even when smiling. His voice had reserves of strength, and many shadings, the sort of voice good talkers have. And again this curious mixture of energy and modesty. Later we would hear people say of him, "Oh yes! He is a Hero of the Soviet Union." Suddenly one was glad to hear the word and to say it. A hero. Perhaps we don't acknowledge them as existing, and surely give them no badge.

Philippe had been asked by the Russians in Paris whether he would like to shoot. "I first want to know what they shoot," said Philippe. Today's host said he had had a good day's hunting the Sunday before, but the walking had been a little long, twenty miles in the snow up to here. "Up to here" was breast high.

He started to speak of bear hunting. My own relationship to bears is exceedingly limited, but I think you would like to hear this. The bear sleeps in his cave, sealed in by the snow, settled for the winter. The air comes into the cave through the hollow trunk of a dead tree, which acts somewhat like a smokestack. Some scent recognizable to the dogs hovers near the tree trunk. The dogs seek it and start to bark. The bear turns in his sleep. When the dogs keep on barking, he becomes enraged. He hates the dogs and their barking and this eruption into his sleep. To stop them, he slowly staggers his way out of the cave. The sportsmen have been set in a wide circle around the tree.

The skin of the gray bear is rather beautiful.

The only bears I have ever seen were in zoos eating fish that were too small for them.

꧁

When we were in Leningrad we had talked several times on the telephone with Elsa Triolet. Both she and her husband, Louis Aragon, were staying with her sister, Lili Brik, in Moscow.

(Once, I mentioned to Elsa over the telephone that the girl interpreters were charming, geographically efficient, but that they had the slimmest notions of history, and that I would have to wait till I got to France or to Japan to find out a little more about the national hero Alexander Nevski. It is perhaps thanks to Elsa that things changed, in a sense, and that we were given, as our interpreter-guide in Moscow, the enchanting and intelligent computer expert, Margot.)

Philippe has always had the most affectionate admiration for Aragon.

Aragon, elegant, moody-eyed, would mock at his fellow men if it weren't for an extreme sensitivity which somehow forbids this. He is the recognized intellectual head of the French Communist party, and his following among the young and the Left everywhere in Europe is immense. One of the two greatest writers in France, "if not the greatest," according to those who disagree with him most.

Elsa Triolet, as French as a Russian can ever become, is a delightful novelist in her own right. Aragon compares her writing to a singing voice. Fluid, melodious. She is as at ease in her style as a fish in the Seine. Her eyes are *Les Yeux d'Elsa.*

When I met them, I became at once their slave, though owning a slave might be against their principles.

We would not get to Moscow in time to see them. Elsa, with her usual generous heart, told her sister, Lili Brik, that we would be in Moscow.

Two Russian women, two sisters, just out of their early youth and beginning their beauty at the eve of the Revolution. They were like two young mirrors held up to the brilliant new talents that had started their own upheavals a few years before.

As in a grave and beautiful dance, the two become four.

One is Lili Brik, to whom the great Russian poet Mayakovski speaks incessantly in his poems.

When you consider that in all Mayakovski's poems the theme breaks and turns to Lili Brik (from the first recognition to the suicide death-message: Lili, love me), that in Aragon's poetry and prose there runs like a tide the murmur of his love for Elsa, and that there are other works by less requited admirers, all this translated into many languages, then surely these two sisters have been more written about, more written to, more described than any other women since the Celtic imagination invented Iseult.

While still in their teens, they became poet- and writer-finders the way some people are water-finders.

We went up to the fifth floor to see Lili Brik. A face upturned to greet you, and immediately the golden eyes absorb you. In the "Flute of Vertebrae," Mayakovski describes her as made-up, redheaded, a small face. She must have worn a great deal of make-up when very young, or when others used little or none, because the word *maquillée* comes back and back about her. "For a long time I was obsessed," wrote Elsa, sailing from Russia in the summer of 1918 with their mother, in a year of famine, "by Lili's face as I had seen it on the wharf: the red-haired head thrown back, her wide made-up mouth . . . the eyes the color of chestnuts, very round, luminous, illuminating a face of intense almost excessive expressiveness." This is an actress's face.

It might be a description of Duse's. Now, the mouth is a little smaller, that is the only difference.

And always, the Russian gentleness. There is about Lili Brik a quick, flickering radiance like that of fireflies. Never much seriousness, except for the all-important business of life: people and the words they use. And the words they write with.

The room is narrow. So narrow that the table is pulled out a little from the wall so that two can slip in between the wall and the table; the others sit around the outer side. Some caviar, and then a mushroom soup covered with fresh herbs that gave off a light scent was brought in by an old woman, her vague shape wrapped in several printed cottons, with steel-rimmed glasses on her nose. She examined us carefully, and since she smiled, I think we passed the examen. A great reader, said Lili, with a little wave. Lili sat at the end of the table and served everyone in turn in the Russian way, with rapid, small gestures. There was some white and some red wine, and nice meat ordered by telephone that morning from Moscow's great big store, the GUM (whose windows show mannequins of young men in evening dress, very Brooks Brothers, but I did not meet with these in the flesh). And a cake possibly; by then we were too absorbed in the conversation to notice.

"How did you survive the Revolution?" asked Philippe.

"We were so happy," Lili answered. *"Nous étions si heureux.* And swollen with hunger."

There is a poem by Mayakovski about her face changing shape.

We have all known listeners, but never a listener such as this. She listens when she is not even looking at you, not turned toward you, a habit of the body.

The dark-red hair is parted in the center, a single plait folded over several times and held at the back of the neck by a brown satin ribbon. When she tires of this, she lets the plait down, straight down her back, the way young girls' hair is always plaited here, and sits forward, folding and smoothing the brown satin ribbon between her fingers and the edge of her knee.

The telephone rang repeatedly, people asking if they could come. Others would arrive. The small hall, with three rooms leading off it, filled up with coats, fur hats, boots.

Andrei Vosnesensky, the poet, kept walking in and out. He has a broad, slightly turned nose of the sort travelers should have, and a large, flat, pleasant, rather sensual mouth. He decided to sit down and read some poems, or, rather, scan them rhythmically. There was a poem about some women snow-bathing in Siberia, evoking with rapture bright-pink backs, thighs, arms, and breasts, flesh appearing and disappearing in the snow.

Eisenstein

One afternoon the actor Cherkasov came in. He was offered lunch and accepted. It was then half past four. No one was surprised. He had played Ivan the Terrible and Alexander Nevski in Eisenstein's films. We asked what it was like working for Eisenstein. "It was like having the bones removed from one's body. He would say do this, do that, you would think it impossible to do. Physically impossible. But you did it." The hands and shoulders and the whole of his long frame moved as would the rag of an actor body, twisted by Eisenstein's will.

No wonder their art descends straight from the Byzantine. Its figures, hieratic and intensely looming, are drawn up by will, not by bones. Their power lies in the structure of the mind, not of the bones.

The Miser

We saw Cherkasov later playing the Covetous Knight in Pushkin's short play. Alone on the stage with his treasure before him, he gave you the feeling of something fragile and temporary about gold (the fragility of all things that can be taken away) and he put a slow, ineffable bliss and gentleness into the handling of it.

"I know the ecstasy of the murderer, when his knife first plunges into the flesh of the murdered," says the Miser as he touches his gold. Pushkin seems very close to some latter-day confessions.

"The House Where We Lived"

Lili Brik said to us one day, "I would like to take you to the Mayakovski museum. The house where we lived, Mayakovski and I and Ossip Brik." We stopped by for her. The three of us sat in a rickety taxi we had picked up. She told a story as if in questions, with a sort of fresh, tender surprise. She told of the time when she did not yet know Mayakovski. He had come to see her sister, Elsa. Their parents strongly disapproved of these young Futurists who wore extravagant clothes, top hats, and lipstick. So the two sisters had gone out of doors to meet him. While Elsa went for a walk with Mayakovski, Lili sat on a bench and waited. It started to rain, slightly but steadily. To avoid any parental questioning, she sat on. After what seemed to her a very long time, the two returned, delighted with their walk, effervescent. Lili told Mayakovski that should he come to Petrograd, where the Briks were then living, they would be delighted to see him. He came one day, rang the bell, and stayed for fifteen years.

"What about Mr. Brik?"

"He had his own life, but he wanted to live with us."

The Futurists had turned literature upside down. They were in advance of the Revolution by some five years. When Mayakovski at twenty-two walked into the stronghold of almost magical talents around Lili Brik and her sister—Khlebnikov, the Russian Joyce, Shklovsky,* Roman Jacobson, Pasternak—they liked him so much they were afraid to hear his poetry. One night after he read his poems, the emotion was intense. Here it was, a new voice, the voice of their time. He was to become the Poet of the Revolution, drawing great crowds. There was no problem for him: "It was *my* revolution."

Upstairs was the small apartment, today a museum, into which they had moved after the outbreak of the Revolution: the giant Mayakovski, Lili Brik, Ossip Brik, and a medium-sized dog. "You see, nothing superfluous. That was the way one wanted to live then."

Built-in sofa seats covered in cotton stripes. At an angle in the center, the table at which one ate and talked. Over the sofa, on a high shelf, there were no books then, but pots of flowers which Mayakovski would bring. Next door, in an even smaller

* Victor Shklovsky, *The Sentimental Journey* (named after Sterne's novel), *Zoo, or Letters That Do Not Speak of Love*. Roman Jacobson, the linguist. With Velimir Khlebnikov, a poet-philologist, these writers gave priority to new forms, notwithstanding their extraordinary, sensitive talents and total independence of thought. None of this applies to the works of Sholokhov, 1965 Nobel Prize winner, to whom I prefer the author of *Uncle Tom's Cabin*.

room, his desk, with the different-colored inks he used for his poems.

"Teach the heart the feast of the body," said Mayakovski.

One morning in winter, he had brought back

> For my love
>   like a visitor
> I come bringing
>   the rarest things in all of Russia
> Two carrots
>   held up by their green tails
> And one half-log
>   of birchwood.

There was a moment of such clearness and purity of regret that one could ask anything.

"Why did he kill himself?"

"Because he could not bear to grow old. He was haunted by this. He killed himself in a room he had taken to work in, near his newspaper, and where he occasionally stayed. We were in Berlin. He had tried once before."

He had spoken of suicide in several of his poems "How easy the trial voyage would be," this "putting the final stop to a line with a bullet."

There had been struggles and pettiness around him, the poison and jealousy that one finds around every great figure. His strength was such, and his taste for fighting so great, that indeed in this death there was no abdication.

Pasternak, his friend, wrote an elegy and described the mourners, the whole of the great city, those who came to gaze at him after his death at thirty seven. He paid him the tribute he would have liked: "You lay there looking as you said you wished to look, only twenty-two. For the second time, you leapt with the strength of your long legs, straight into the legends of the young."

Downstairs in the museum library were the huge posters, cubist and futuristic in design, that Mayakovski drew for the workers of the Revolution, a sort of chronological history of its needs. Lenin asked the Futurists to decorate Moscow for the first anniversary of the Revolution. "Holy Lord," said an old woman, "what new devils are they making us worship?"

In some photographs Mayakovski had close-cropped hair, or his head is shaved; in others, longish hair. "When he was in a bad humor and things were going wrong, he would let his hair grow," said Lili Brik. "When he was in a good humor he would cut it short, or shave it."

On certain days, Mayakovski would take a few lines from a poet, perhaps Pushkin, or someone of his own time, like Akhmatova, and repeat them, repeat them, aloud or to himself, these fragments of verse, like a litany, a prayer to his private saints.

The great director Meyerhold staged *Mystery-Bouffe, The Bedbug,* and *The Baths.* "They were not really good for each other, Meyerhold and Mayakovski," said Lili Brik. "They respected each other too much. The mistake of the one would be blurred over by the other. This was unsatisfactory."

Two students of Mayakovski's work looked up at her. In the library, a woman, evidently the curator, and a younger one, a helper, stopped her and put some questions to her with infinite respect.

On one wall a huge poster of Lili's face. The same photograph Mayakovski used as a cover for his book *Of This.* Of Love.

The Hare

Russians, Aragon says, have a special word for the spot of sun thrown on a wall by a boy with a piece of mirror in his hand, or light on water mirrored back, even the flash of headlights on a road or a field. A "hare," they say, using the same word for the moving trembling spot as for the animal. Mayakovski, in one of his poems, watches this bright furry spot on a prison wall, when he is in jail, a very young prisoner. Aragon, in a remarkable poem of his own, tells of his discovery in Mayakovski of this word, how it pleases him, how he rejects the "scared like a hare," a proverb current in France: "The hare runs on, his heart beats, ah how it beats, until sometimes he could die. I would have said courageous like a hare. For us who have no word to distinguish, from any fugitive light, this jumping halo, let us at least have this, let the hare be an image."

There is another hare I happened on (not being a serious reader, but opening and shutting books to catch quickly the surprises they hold). This hare is in St. Augustine, in a short story against the "vehement desire of the eyes." "If by chance," he tells us, "I ride through a field and see a dog running after a hare, I become so absorbed in the pursuit, that I forget even my deepest thoughts. My heart is pulled along."

In Aragon the hare's scent leads to the writer: "I thought, in this time of adventure and sound . . . that in the smoke, I had gesticulated, one could think me an actor in the play, but I say this to you: I gave the most of my time to the passage of the image to the word, of the word to the image, to and fro. I admit this. I blame myself to have distracted any of the human time allowed me for anything else but the passage of word to image."

This mastery was never more apparent than in Aragon's novel *La Mise à Mort. The Kill,* perhaps that is the way he would want it translated. The words cover the moment of the bull's death, decision and act, the tragedy in the bull ring. It also means an execution. The book, a sort of summing up of man's pain, doubts, hopes, and delights, using several different forms, was like a fire in a field, renewing the language and the novel. For some, it became obsessional. A man's life and more.

The pain of living it, the sensuous joy of telling it. After the book appeared, young writers kept quoting him, halting a sentence to do so, speaking to him, addressing him in their own work.

Aragon has invented a type of colloquial writing, a conversation with the reader, sometimes cool, sometimes enormous and violent, bridging, or, rather, erasing, the difference between speaking and writing. As a poet's colloquy, it carries you on no ordinary journey. The young man, the great man, the Sybil, the dervish drunk in ecstasy, the wounded in each of us, speak in their sleep. In sleep, because the dialogue is thrust upon you. In sleep, so close is the voice, could someone listen.

I have before me a paperback, his autobiography, *The Unfinished Novel*, written in verse and prose. He is the man who says of himself, "O madman who nevertheless had gone off in search of another life, O crusader of a modern dream . . . of heaven knows what America, what land, what monastery. You, holding out your hand to people who do not want it, listen to this, one more time, listen: if ever other men look at you as though you were one of their own it will be an illusion, a trap, a semblance."

The tide subsides. The same man, when he speaks of trees, of rain, of light, of flowers, turns spontaneously to Elsa: "You are the air that brought to me light pollens."

"Nothing else but my love over everything like a shadowy lime tree, nothing else but my love."

There is a line just before the conclusion, the sixth line before the ending: "The surprise when the other touches you."

Later on, in Paris, Lili Brik was sitting with her husband, Vasili Katanyan, her sister, Elsa Triolet, and her brother-in-law, Louis Aragon. And ourselves. We were having a delicious tea. Aragon sat quietly eating bread and butter, looking pleased with his guests, or perhaps with the tea. Lili said someone had questioned her as to which were her favorite words. "What are my favorite words?" she said. She looked around the room, first at her sister, then at her brother-in-law, and said in a light, slow voice ". . . Elsa, Louis, Revolution . . ."

Ossip Brik

Ossip Brik, Lili's first husband, was a technician of literature. He wrote some very interesting essays on the Formalists, the brilliant writers' group of his time. He had the sort of structured mind that could give cohesive meaning to new forms and new attempts and help make them into a movement.

This is a story that to me illustrates the difference between the Russian reaction to seemingly unalterable events and what ours might be.

Ossip Brik's parents were millionaires. "Not big millionaires," said Lili, "but millionaires." His father, at the beginning of the Revolution, made an arrangement with his bank. A certain sum, not very large, but still adequate to cover his needs, was to be allowed him at regular intervals. One day, he went to the bank, and was told there would no longer be any money forthcoming. He would receive nothing whatsoever. "This is impossible," said Ossip Brik's father. "I gave you my confidence." "And what does your confidence matter to us?" asked the young man in the bank.

Ossip Brik's father went home to tell the story. "Why should my confidence matter to him?" he commented. "He is quite right."

This is probably an example of what is meant by the Russian capacity, or gift, for accepting and immersing themselves

in events larger than ordinary life. It is unthinkable for an An-
glo-Saxon to behave in this manner on hearing such news from
his bank.

Basins

Once, at Lili Brik's, we had a sample of the futuristic views
of the Mayakovski days. Philippe was asked if we were comfortable in our hotel. One thing, he answered, puzzled him.
Why had water basins in the bathroom no stoppers whatever?
Bathtubs, yes, but not basins. We had been warned and had
brought our own, but it might improve things for tourists if
some stoppers were provided. Someone said this never oc-
curred to Russians; they liked to wash their hands with the water
running. "It would be simpler," concluded Lili Brik, "if all the
hotels outside of Russia took out their stoppers."

The Sin against Human Dignity

One morning, one dreadful morning, I committed the sin
against human dignity. My breakfast had been three quarters
of an hour in coming; people would soon be waiting downstairs. The tea appeared. No toast. Another quarter of an hour
and the waiter came carrying a dish, which he put down on the
table, and shuffled away. Under the napkin lay four slices of
raw bread. I lifted the napkin, saw the bread, and something
happened. Across the room flew the dish, the napkin, the bread.
I didn't know anyone could throw that fast. A cry of horror
came out of me. The old waiter stopped short. Both the waiter
and I instantaneously lifted our hands to each other in prayer.

"Excuse me, excuse me—*Izveeneetié, izveeneetié,*" we repeated to each other. Less than five minutes later, hot toast arrived, delicious. Philippe during the whole scene pretended not to know me. He was obviously deciding how best to separate himself from these wild capitalistic goings-on. "I didn't think that you were behaving quite as you should," he said later.

The Women in the Street

The women in the street are holding their noses to keep them from freezing, a sure sign the temperature has dropped.

I can never get over the surprise of seeing Russians, on days without wind, stop to talk to each other as the snow is falling, with obvious enjoyment. Someone told Monroe Wheeler that the snow was a liberation to them, as early summer is to Americans. The snow makes the whole of the country one surface, quiet, swift, smooth. Everything is possible; it is the time when you can go everywhere with ease.

There is in the air an energetic laziness.

If you get on a bus or a streetcar and have no money, you don't have to pay.

A workman's rent today is five per cent of his salary. They plan in the next seven years to reduce it to nothing.

Plisetskaya

We went to see Plisetskaya dance, taken by two charming Russian friends. He of the thin, darker-eyed variety of Russians. She also dark, but of stronger build, with a warm straightforwardness. She had tied a scarlet chiffon scarf around her head, the ends reaching down to the hem of her coat. (For the street you remove your small fur, merely decorative, and put on a warm wool coat such as her red one.)

We lost ourselves for hours in the contemplation of Pliset-skaya's arms, their uncanny length, more like armatures for wings. The make-up of the entire skin of a dancer is pale pink; on the stage this takes on a sort of light. Plisetskaya's thin arms would flutter on, past the needs of the music and the story, bird free; her body, when Juliet dances for Romeo, like a bird's body, of secondary importance to these radiant whirrings.

Plisetskaya came to Paris to dance for Picasso's eightieth birthday. We saw her at a party. Her dark eyes enchanted, and she was wearing the dress she had bought that morning. The next day I went out and bought the very same. It was wool of a brilliant turquoise color, with incrustations at the top of gold and silver, like lozenges. One could put on harlequin-patterned silver stockings, flat-heeled transparent shoes, and have a lovely time.

We walked home from the Bolshoi with our Russian friends. In the street, we talked before saying good night, and for some reason, just at the end, both of them spoke of Kennedy. Our friend's wife turned to me. "We wept here when he died," she said.

Ira Aldridge

A hundred years before, in the theater across the way, the American Negro actor Ira Aldridge had played for a season. His two great parts were King Lear and Othello. Seats were impossible to get, and at each performance the applause was interminable. Some of the audience thought he was too restrained and that he "roared reasonably" as Othello. For King Lear, he wore heavy white make-up, except for his hands, which, through coquetry, he wore bare and brown.

I Will Live to See the Day

The Minister of Culture, Madame Furtseva, was kind enough to receive us. She is a very charming woman—strong straight legs, blond, a direct glance—and has done a great job of exporting Russian theater and sending young and gifted intellectuals to foreign lands, so that one could look at them and enjoy them.

We wanted to know something of Russia's future plans for new museums. They were to open a new Tretiakov museum, replacing the old one, in 1967. This would be important. The conversation wandered and became fascinating. Theater, the Russian woman, children, education, new decisions in government spending, et cetera. Then the direct glance swept Philippe. Hand on the heart she said: "I hope, I do hope, I will live to see the day when you too will live in a true democracy."

There are quite a few differences in vocabulary to get accustomed to. Plisetskaya is not considered "lyrical." She is not a lyrical dancer, they say. Ehrenburg speaks of Shakespeare's verse as being "realistic." The head waitress in the hotel told us that we were *very* cultured, meaning that we had relatively good manners.

Tonight, in Griboedov's famous play *The Misfortune of Being Clever*, first printed in 1833, characters say to one another: "What? Educate them? Why they are no better than beasts, I tell you, no better than beasts." Griboedov was an ambassador, and took time out to note the casual chatter he heard at home. A hundred and thirty years later, they have educated themselves into something resembling a folly of education.

This they believe: that they have added a new dimension of dignity to man. They are at ease in their skins.

The importance of the individual, which we find a necessity and wish to defend with our lives, is to them negligible, almost an error in taste.

The quickest way to get put into prison, and if it is proved, to be kept there, is to commit a crime "against human dignity." Because the State guarantees the dignity of all, personal dignity becomes negligible when face to face with the State, small out of all proportion. Errors, human pain, are natural costs. A sort of taxation of the spirit, for the good of the many.

For this good, they absolve the government from past mistakes and therefore future ones, if I have understood correctly.

Zagorsk

We were going to the country to see Zagorsk. The isbas on either side of the road looked the way the traveler has seen them for hundreds of years: weather-beaten logs or clapboard, with lacy frames carved around their windows, painted. No more than two or three rooms each, far smaller than the huge trucks ceaselessly passing them. Then we would be between lines of frozen-over trees that were perhaps poplars, the iced snow giving them the look of glowing pear trees.

In front of us, a chalk-white wall rising from the snow.

Within, nine, perhaps fifteen, churches of different colors: this was the Monastery of St. Serge, in Zagorsk, which includes Troitski Cathedral, the Trinity.

We wandered about, the temperature thirty-five degrees centigrade below zero, the sun shining. A line of Spenser's, which Philippe had translated, kept turning in my mind: "But this— the work of heart's astonishment." The outside of the refectory was a swirl of columns, green succeeding to green, red succeeding to white, orange to red. Was it the colors or ourselves shivering in an orchard? "He bringeth forth divers fruits, and flowers of many colors, and grass."

The priests walk furiously in and out of the closed doors that partition off the altar, swinging incense or chanting in full and rapid voices, like warriors. Along the sides of the church, women fling themselves against the ground, kiss it, get up, go to the next icon, again fling themselves down.

We met several priests. We were taken in to a delicious lunch. As usual, brandy was drunk at the beginning. We had caviars of several different colors, sweet-and-sour cucumbers, an elderly veal, and some little cakes.

Our interpreter, an unquestioning atheist, behaved at first a little like a great lady taken to night spots where she shouldn't be seen. Polite, but indifferent. But there was one man who impressed her so much that she would later say, "I didn't know there was anyone like that." He was Father Philarete, the young head of the Department of Theology. (Two hundred men are in training at Zagorsk, one of the three largest of the religious universities.) He had the strong smooth face of a young lioness and a dark friendly glance from under long straight lashes. We returned later on to see him, not only because of his charm and youth and looks, but because of another quality. After a while spent with him, one got the feeling that he was after something he would be a long time in reaching, but that life was long, and that he had the time, and the will, and was very patient. Life is long, and at the end of it, for some, lies saint-hood.

Our Father Nicolas knew Father Philarete. They had gone to school together. Orthodox priests and deacons have wives; monks take the celibate's vows. Father Nicolas had hoped that his friend would not become a monk, would not take his vows of celibacy. He knew a very beautiful girl and had brought her to his friend. "After three weeks, he returned the girl," said Father Nicolas. Vocations sometimes leap over the bodies of friends.

We talked a long time. At one moment he expressed his feel-ing that outsiders had false ideas of the religious life.

"You see," he said, "the presence of God is a joyous one. The meals in the refectory are very gay. We in our convent are not sad. We may not have what you have, but there is no grief. We have something else, or, rather, someone else. There is a differ-ence."

"Were you lucky? Was it easy for you, this decision, this re-nunciation, or at least what it implies of renunciation?"

The face became serious, absolutely quiet. Then the answer: "Is anything easy?"

"Have you ever regretted?" we asked.

"Never."

Window Dressing

The big cities are the true paradise of window dressers. They are dressed once for as long as the season lasts, whatever that may be. Nothing in the window can be moved or changed, or sold.

I saw some coats which looked just like the children's clothes of Buckingham Palace, but somehow prettier, and I wanted to bring them back for Philippine's Camille and little Philippe. But I remembered that the store had probably exhausted its stock, and nothing would ever make the remaining coats leave the windows.

Displays in the country stores show a great difference from those of a city. The blight of poorly garnished shelves: what is there does not seem wanted.

Restaurants

The restaurants are always too big, too high. The only pleasant ones are Caucasian, split up into smaller rooms, in one of which sits a Georgian orchestra making sounds fit for purgatory. A table of young Georgians will start to sing, not the melodious sounds (at least to my ears) of Chinese or Japanese No music, but a ghastly rasping noise, just a little off key. They rise to drink to the last drop the wine poured into a large fruit bowl.

The Georgians are great spenders. They own their land in Georgia and come up to the cities to sell their private produce, oranges and the like. They have dark, curly hair, are strong and loud, and have a reputation for adoring women. They rather flaunt this amiable predilection for women, but not to the point of bringing them to restaurants.

These restaurants are extremely popular with Russians, and they should be, since they are by far the best and the most fun. The food is good. Roasted and marinated lamb, the best pink or black caviar, good rice, and ices. Caucasian bread is brought in looking like flat, limp pieces of bedsheets, and is delicious when eaten hot with butter. Its only drawback is that, made without yeast, it swells inside of you with disturbing rapidity.

Quantities of cut glass give the table a festive look. Table linen has not caught up with the demand. When you are a foreigner you rate, sometimes, a fresh tablecloth. If not, you pick out the table with the fewest spots.

What takes some of the amusement out of dining are the menus—printed like vows, once and forever, and absolutely alike for every restaurant in Russia. Making a profit on food is disdained, worse, considered distasteful. A pity, because it probably would improve its taste. When you are with Russians you always eat very well; they know how and what to choose.

The only time I saw Philippe rebel was in Kiev. "I am willing," he said to the uncomprehending but charmed waitress, "to cope with necks of chickens, but see no reason to eat the *nails* [*sic*]."

Embassies

If you live in Moscow, it is better not to belong to an embassy. If you do, you live in purdah, communicating with Russians rarely, if at all.

There was a sort of ghetto for embassies in Ivan the Terrible's day. The suspicion toward the foreign envoy continues.

We saw houses built in the bad period before 1917 by the *nouveau-riche* merchants, such as the house that shelters the French Embassy in Moscow. They mostly look as though they had been raised by happy and wanton dogs, mixing their styles, and rollicking about for the fun of it. Two merchants bought the Matisses now in the Hermitage and the Gauguins in the Pushkin. Who else in Europe was asking Matisse before 1912 to paint a nude dance for his family hall?

There was another museum director to whom we had a letter—V. Gouber, of the Pushkin. We sent the letter around with a little note, telephoned, and duly arrived one morning at the museum. An English friend, the editor of an English art magazine, had said before giving us the letter, "Ah Gouber," and sighed with pleasure.

We sat and waited for him in a small room, hesitant as to where to leave all the layers that we were bundled into—coats, sweaters, furs, boots. Whether to even start this peeling process. It is very difficult to greet someone for the first time half in and half out of a recalcitrant coat, with a somewhat wet fur hat in your hand, one boot off, and the other on, and not feel that this new relationship is beginning in utter disorder.

Gouber looked surprisingly tall, with the endless legs of a cavalry officer. He was blue-eyed, his straight blond hair was parted on the side, barely graying. We knew him to be near the age of retirement, but still busy with the museum life, exhibitions, publications, and, because he loved to teach, art classes.

The tour was delightful. Gouber and Philippe lingered near some radiant, opalescent skin: a Renoir knee-length portrait of a woman in blue. Farther on, Philippe seemed just as fascinated by a nice, but not especially surprising, chest of drawers. This because of a little sentence of Gouber's: "We bought this commode a short while ago from a collector." Collectors again.

At last, the Gauguins.

The Gauguins of the Pushkin are to Moscow what the Matisses of the Hermitage are to Leningrad. The youth of Matisse is enclosed in the northern city. The measure of Gauguin's greatness, whatever and wherever the pictures one has seen before, is somehow here in the Pushkin.

Two rooms, wall after wall of Gauguins. But are there any

walls? You turn, there is a copper body, or one the color of tobacco leaves; and there went out another who was red, as John
said in Revelation. Leaves, sometimes blue, or black, and of
some bright substance that in other painters is called green, with
the inner sheen of fur. A metamorphosis is taking place. The
trees, the women, are rendered as animals, and these shapes,
half-shadows, half-beings, are their work.

Such fare could hardly have been given to the good-looking,
prim Danish woman he married, who thought she was to share
the life of someone working in a bank.

The bodies are often superimposed like collages. On one can-
vas, a title is painted in Polynesian. The words, we are told,
mean "Confidences." Two women are sitting with their backs
turned to us. A pool of black hair and a pool of blue shadows,
brown shoulders above a cloth of intense pink in the center.
And quiet.

Philippe's and Gouber's footsteps could be heard returning
to fetch me.

We asked Gouber to dine with us. He was free the following
Tuesday, and we took him to the Caucasian restaurant. In the
lull of the screeching music, after the pink caviar, always so
fresh, Philippe asked Gouber how, bearing a famous liberal name
of pre-Revolutionary Russia (not necessarily the guarantee of a
safe passport to the Bolsheviks), he had come through the Revolution to the directorship of the Pushkin. "It was quite simple,"
said Gouber. "I was a young soldier, and went straight over to
the Revolutionary troops."

The words made present before our eyes the day when
throughout Leningrad the bright red cockades were being
pinned on the coats of soldiers and officers alike, as one by one,
the regiments went over to the side of the new. Everywhere the
young men were rallying. At the time, people thought that
there might be an abdication, and a new government headed

by a member of the Tsar's family, brother or cousin. One could still see the grand dukes' cars with the imperial fanion speeding back and forth through the city streets.

Night Visitors

Up to the middle of the nineteenth century, during the cold of the winter some of the streets in Moscow were barred with wooden palisades. Against the wolves, who came at night.

The Ideal Bookcase

Maurice Baring wrote somewhere that the ideal bookcase would be one into which you could plunge your hand in the dark and bring out something you wanted to read.

The Russian mind is like that.

They are much aware of another vague region, no one's birthplace, ambiguous and ambivalent, called the soul. If you could plunge in your hand you would surely pull out something of great service that would shine for you or comfort you in more difficult or emptier moments.

Questions

There were certain questions that we could not ask, because some questions implied a certain criticism. Voluntary or involuntary, this might be well received one moment, not at another.

We were very careful, because we wanted to be trusted, wanted our thoughts to be trusted, above all we wanted to be friends. Leave the criticisms and the carpings to others. The defect inherent in their system—the danger of a power that admits no criticism—they knew. They knew more examples than we could ever sense.

The Party

The Communist party numbers five per cent of the Soviet citizens. It is more a vocation than a pleasure. Its demands are very great. Absolutely necessary if you are planning a political career, it becomes a halter in private life and can disorganize you. If you are a promising young doctor, for instance, just as the number of your patients is increasing, you can be sent to a kolkhoz, or any sort of farm land, because the government needs agricultural help. Also, if you are dropped from the party for some reason, either obstreperous behavior or normal unworthiness, doors close. Members of the party are admired, but not envied.

I asked why one nice woman we knew, of no great interest, wished to become a member of the party. "Because she is stupid," came the answer.

The Unspoken

There were some tacit accords. Some subjects were taboo. They did not question me about the riots in Chicago, the marches, our Mississippi governors. I did not question them about who, in their literary world, would next be sent to a labor camp.

The war in Vietnam was never discussed with me, only with Philippe. Because of some sort of tact or some sort of politeness, they forebore questioning me. What could I have said had they asked? Turned away, or answered, as all good Americans do in foreign countries: "It is very difficult. We would like to find some solution. We are doing our best." This best, applied year after year, seems hardly sufficient. We go on counting the dead. Perhaps one should answer: This is but the beginning of a long war with China. A heritage we are preparing to leave our own. Or add firmly that we like to "deliver" small nations from Communism. Small nations. Otherwise? Otherwise, when a Communist nation has become strong, we work out a treaty.

Outside the largest, most up-to-date hotels throughout the world, Teheran, Tokyo, Paris, Stockholm, wherever an American statesman is staying, crowds are filing past with banners. "Murderers." It is nothing, the spectator is told, nothing but an orderly manifestation by the students and the Left. "U.S.A. Murderers."

It is perhaps nothing, but the young are there. Some of the men in our colleges might also choose to be shouting in the street below. The young men will go home, and grow up. But what of ourselves?

Never did so many feel so in need of the young.

Everyone is convinced of our strength. It is what we are doing with it that scares the informed and uninformed alike. They find a contradiction between what we say and what we do. Sometimes our newspapers present us to ourselves in a dismaying light. At the beginning of a dispatch from Cu-Chi, signed by one of our best and most read correspondents, one finds this: "One of the most interesting trends in Vietnam is the progressive division of the U.S. army into pacifiers, and the big unit-killers. Most divisions perform both functions, but you invariably find that one function is strongly preferred to the other. The 1st Division for instance became a champion big unit-killer. To be sure the 1st Division is using its resources for a vastly successful pacification project that has the VC on the run. But despite its success, the men of Big Red One still prefer big unit-killing."

This year we will spend as usual, Philippe and I, a month in Majorca. There we will see what you do not see in Russian waters: superb American ships, sometimes an atomic carrier, putting in. At night, strings of light bulbs edge their high shapes. The young men who stride about and scan the menus in *bistros* are products of the atomic age, their niceness immediate, and in their vocabulary sudden terms of the great know-how necessary for their jobs. Amid the small quick Mediterranean people, they seem strangely foreign.

Later at night, the new Barbarians, rich, huge, and drunken, wander off toward the shores where their ships are waiting. They have forgotten the delicate electronic insides of their boats. They totter to and fro along the walls, watched from corner to corner by military police, by then indulgent and tired.

Young men much like these are having their apprenticeship in Vietnam. They will fight an enemy who wants very much what they want: a home, food, money enough, better education. Sometime, somewhere, safety. "I live with bread like you, feel want, taste grief, need friends," wrote Paulinus to his tutor Ausonius.

There is a moment in a long war when the killed become indistinguishable from the killers.

Better pretend there are no questions, each left to his own brooding. At best, less than a sentence, more prayer than statement: all Americans are concerned.

There is an interesting little game to be played during quiet evenings: take an almanac and add up the world's populations in two columns, one entitled Capitalists, the other Communists. Over half the world's population comes under the second heading. Will we be able to settle our differences by force? We will need firm hearts, and not much good sense.

Watchers

It is curious what a good interpreter makes of you. You become an intense watcher, a listener listening just a little too carefully, the way actors do. Two people, the one who just spoke and the one who will be answering, are watching each other's face. Hardly ever the interpreter's. The one is seeking in the other the reason for the words, their other meaning. This gives the conversation a strange leisure, yet tightens it below the surface. At least in Russia.

Invisible Guests

A very odd thing happens in conversation with Russians. It is the presence of what is left *unsaid*. Anglo-Saxons and Latins politely suppress any outward awareness of the subject to be avoided. And again, through courtesy, we try to blot out the unwelcome subject or push it into the back of our mind.

Here, the avoided is frankly present in the conversation. The "quickness of apprehension of the Russian mind," to use Maurice Baring's words, is such that every utterance is keyed to the missing subject. For instance, if a man has just been left by his wife, her name is not mentioned, but her presence is recognized in the conversation as one discusses the pain the children may feel, the drab summer in view. Nothing is passed over by tact, and yet it is so deftly done that an onlooker would never know one had just touched the ghost.

Ostankino

Cherkasov, the actor, introduced us to a woman who had been one of Russia's greatest actresses. Once a known beauty, she now sat in profile in our upper-tier box, intently watching the stage as if the play were already on. All that remained of former feasts was a large timid blue eye. She had loved Paris, which she had known as a young woman, and had last been there in 1935. We talked of our intense pleasure in the quality of Russian taste, its inventiveness, its distinction. (The French having deceived us, as they have deceived the world about much art that is not theirs, by deciding that it was merely bizarre.)

"It is supreme taste," the actress answered. This has also been said of Virgil. And the late eighteenth-century country palaces are like that, Virgilian, the color of the water and the air, fresh with the scent of the country, simpler and purer than elsewhere, yet of the most careful workmanship. Virgilian. Ostankino, Pavlosk, but Ostankino above all.

Prince Sheremetev had two hundred thousand serfs. He obtained from these his silversmiths, cabinetmakers, glass blowers, ironsmiths, gilders. Their workmanship equaled that of the ateliers furnishing the French court. The most gifted were freed by their master to attend the St. Petersburg Art College, where great Russian and foreign masters of art taught them, so that they became architects, designers, creators. Around 1775, at the beginning of the best work of the Louis XVI period, the

Prince built Ostankino. Furniture, decorations, perfume-burners, chandeliers, almost all are still there. Egypt had been discovered, and sphinxes abound, but they are flattened and gray, unobtrusive ghosts of the Egyptians. The rest is of light blues and greens, white and green gold, and the chandeliers of red glass or sapphire blue.

Ostankino at a little distance appears to be made of pale pink stone; close to, you see that it is of wood, carved like blocks, and painted. The outside sculptured draperies and flower garlands are also of wood.

Rooms, simple in appearance, but immensely detailed. Ceilings with carved cornices, young ferns rather than acanthuses, the flower, not the leaf, of lilies of the valley. The lightest of eyes demanded this. The taste is happily bound by the Louis XVI fashions, but nearer the summer fields than the court.

Prince Sheremetev married a serf. The serf had become an actress with a ravishing voice and played in his private theater. The house and theater, its scenery, live happily ever after.

A Sheremetev now resides in Moscow, without a serf, extremely likable, we were told.

The Yussupoffs

The Yussupoff country house is a grand layout of yellow-and-white columned walks around courtyards, the whole thing set in a forest. Inside, it is a stupid house. One Yussupoff had a mania for dark, serious Italian pictures. He made an exception, surprisingly, for a Tiepolo, one of his Cleopatras much as those of the Labia palace, looking overdressed and full of Superbia here. The drawing room and study must have been made charming by the quantities of flowers, the photographs of friends in silver frames, always the same handsome profiles, or people shooting, taken out of doors while they waited for something. Fabergé presents. And the beauty of the Yussupoffs.

"They did not need brains, since they had felicity," once wrote Karen Blixen of the Danish aristocracy.

The Grand Duke Dmitri and Prince Yussupoff were under house arrest in this house after the Rasputin murder.

There is there a small private theater. When you walk in, you have the feeling you are opening a fresh pea pod.

Conspirators

Peter the Great locked up his sister in a convent near Moscow. She had conspired against him. When she looked out of her window she could see across the way the hand of one of her fellow conspirators that Peter had had nailed up on the shutter. We wondered how long one would look at that hand. I believe she never left the convent.

Dmitri

I kept wondering where another convent was, the convent where the Grand Duke Dmitri had stopped during military maneuvers to see his aunt, a nun and the sister of the Emperor. One evening in the South of France, he had told me this story. Foreshortened, as was his way.

His regiment had been riding a long time. It was the end of the day. The air was heavy, copper-colored, and the dust hardly rose. The gray and black crows were sitting in the dust on the ground.

The men at last arrived at the convent, and Dmitri went in

to see his aunt. She and he had supper together. It was probably quickly brought, because the Russians, so slow in public places, are quick when serving an unexpected guest, quick at anything they really wish to do. A strange guest in a country convent, this young officer, whose great looks were famous. They talked a long time. He must have walked to and fro, his head lowered, like a young lion's, in love with talk. She accompanied him to the door when he left. There was about him, they said, something fragile which was his youth, and something shining and compelling which was the quality of his beauty.

She gave him her blessing. "I have a request to make of you," she added. "I ask of you only one thing. Do not, ever, come back."

So great is the grace of nephews, so quickly could the soul lose its quiet.

Vladimir

We were leaving for Vladimir by train to see the Extraordinary. The Extraordinary being the frescoes painted in the fourteenth century by Rublev, a painter who defies all attempts at reproduction.

His paintings, like certain writings, change one. For a time more or less long, but they do change one. I came to experience this several times.

Vladimir was once the capital of Russia. A prince of Kiev, Vladimir the Bright Sun, built a new capital, this small city, where nothing much remains of him but a long white wall and a white cathedral with eleven golden domes. And the Rublev frescoes.

It was near midnight when the train stopped; the Bishop was sending his car. The clergy use the same large black limousines as those that meet travelers, but theirs have curtains. The door of the curtained car opened and down stepped a young man. "He had the face of a god," says Ovid, "but I do not know which god." I knew. This was the lengthened body, the narrow eyes, the short slim nose, the glance that looked at you and widened, the way some lenses do as you peer into them—the face of an archangel of Rublev. The long overcoat and the small gray fur cap were hazards of the century.

One is aware, in the Rublev figures, of something that they know and that you do not know. They have acquired this knowledge, infinitely difficult and precarious, and in so doing have not lost their ability to love. They love as naturally as they wash their long hands in water.

We lost the archangel. While the other members of the party were having a late supper, I went to bed. I was told that he repeatedly asked whether he would be needed the next day. Our interpreter said that we already had a well-informed deacon and that perhaps would be good enough. I thought it odd to tell an archangel that he wasn't needed.

There was no Intourist hotel. In the existing inn the water had a ghastly smell; it was difficult to brush your teeth with it. The Russians told us this water was very good for you, famous for curing kidney ailments. Our apartment had been freshly repainted; the quilts were of the lightest feathers incased in pale-blue satin. The maids were the best we had while in Russia, the equals in thoughtfulness and refinement of the best maids anywhere. The hotel could not always keep up with them. One rushed up, to say, beaming: "Hot water tomorrow afternoon at three o'clock." How nice. But perhaps not the most convenient time.

Suzdal

Suzdal is a quiet, sacred city. Its purity on a winter morning made one long for the government to turn some of the unused old convents into excellent hotels, throughout the country, each somewhat on the idea of the best Spanish *parador*, and furnish them with copies of the furniture in the Naryshkin palace, for the bliss of the traveler and the good of his soul. Occasionally, here and there, white churches or a convent, like feathery geometric birds. Then again the snow and the plain.

The doors of the Cathedral of the Nativity of the Virgin are of dark-green bronze, like the Ghiberti doors in Florence, but the scenes, instead of being sculptured, are etched in gold, to look like icons on a green background.

The Nerl

The snow blocked the road and the bridge, and we could see the church only from afar, where you could not distinguish the river from the land. Arches thrown up as high as an arch can go, that is, as far as a fifth story, filled with a substance thick as milk. On the black roof, a simple onion-shaped dome. In summer the church reflects in the slow-moving Nerl. "In the water, the fish wave their gray cold tails," writes Sosnora, who started as a metal worker and is now one of Russia's most rewarding young poets. A passing note on woman's role: Sosnora's father was a colonel in the reserves, his mother an engineer.

Perhaps the most important part of a journey is what it discovers in you. How suddenly a sentence will surface, how some words printed on a page become yours, yours their power and emotion. How the memory of a person become unfamiliar will slip between you and what you are looking at. How easily two hands cup two bare shoulders. The curve of a wall, a stone imbedded in brick, rough to the touch, tree branches trained into roofs, snow against gold, will bring you nearer to the chosen land of your taste: This is mine.

Because none of us move without this huge baggage which we pretend we have checked, and that on the contrary we are constantly opening, shutting, sorting. Comparing. From one's reading, not whole sentences, but splinters; not smooth words rightly paved, but their uneven surfaces, their feel. The body's memory.

We returned as we came, by one of their broad trains, entirely of aluminum, looking light blue inside, furnished with airplane seats. Small cribs are fastened to the forward end of the car, where mothers can put their traveling babies.

Kiev

We stayed only a day and a half in Kiev, having planned for five.

We had gone to Kiev because of Paustovsky and his description of its leafy trees and public gardens along the Dnieper. But we were in the wrong season. The trees had no leaves as yet, the ground no snow. The cathedral and other churches had been reconstructed after the damage of the war, perhaps too much, or too recently, and held no magic.

However, there was one wall along a curving staircase. Many times, in Istanbul, we had stared at the Hippodrome. Nothing of Byzantium is left around it, nothing but a small earthen racing ground, still inviolate. The gilded horses are in Venice in front of St. Mark's, the two gilded serpents likewise gone. Suddenly, on this very wall, the Emperor and Empress were staring out at us from under the arched windows of the palace wall overlooking the Hippodrome. They were in the pearls and clothes of Ravenna, the court and other notables at smaller windows. Had a painter working in Kiev for Dolgoruki, the Prince of the Long Hand, so regretted Byzantium that he painted this small worldly scene of a racing day on the available space of a little-used stairway?

Publishers

Convents are the only publishers of good art books. Those published by the State are backward in photography, typography, and layout. The convents manage to present thoughtful, elegant editions.

The Vassili Basilica

If you enter the Vassili Basilica, near Lenin's tomb, through a side door, a wall suddenly blocks your path, a painted wall.

Matisse was in Moscow in 1911, invited by one of his patrons. Some of his backgrounds to women—white, patterned with red flowers outlined in black, with the curves of their long black stems almost circular—here they are in front of you.

Matisse was evidently as startled by this wall as we are.

The Tomb

The young men are across the way, filing slowly through Lenin's tomb. They go to stare at the energy of the man who in seven short years changed Russia into the U.S.S.R. Only seven short years and the young men are still filing past.

Love one another, said the Gospels. Help one another, lend your hands to one another. Be aware, be present, said Lenin.

For years, there was misery. Then it was so terrifyingly *even,* so long-lasting, that to some it appeared to be endemic. And now, they are living a miracle. The thick gold is on the domes again. (The gold put on like large squares of gold plate, as a traveler in the seventeenth century has already remarked.) They have the cosmos—small high-heeled shoes for the women, thick pale-blue carpet in the supper room of their theater.

It is a society which has solved many of its problems on its own terms, where the scientists have the social privileges of English dukes, the musicians, those of rebellious but very well-looked-after younger sons. Privileges go with each profession. Over all this there is still the very young spirit of "we are trying to do something better together."

No one is excluded except, perhaps, the writer.

This seems a contradiction, since in no country do writers and poets have a wider public. Twelve thousand strong listen to Vosnesensky and Yevtushenko, and other young poets. But talent depends also on choice of subject, and on form. When it comes to those, the State is jealous.

The most dangerous of all careers is that of writer. Since the beginning of Russian literature, his path leads to exile, deportation, police-surveyed sojourns in distant provinces, death. Things have not much changed since the tsars. In biographies of poets and writers who gave their faith and talent to the Revolution, these are the more than occasional sentences one reads: "Died in Siberia." "Died in the train returning from Siberia." Died "under a cloud." "Was shot." "Was shot." Years in labor camps may, or may not, change a man.

And yet, as a writer needs a public and as Russians are the best possible public and the most sensitive, the writer goes out to meet it, proud of its understanding and uncertain of his fate.

"A writer?" says Musil. "Who can ever be sure to have caught one alive?"

Skinning and Paring Words

You can almost feel the surge of pent-up talents ready to burst forth. In music, in writing, in painting. (Architecture would take a special commentary, since inventive modern architecture is almost nonexistent. But they should one day use glass, with their sense of greens and blues, as it has never yet been used.)

In writing, the renewal has already taken place. The young men and women have followed in the footsteps of the great revolutionaries of writing, the giants, those who were in their twenties and thirties at the time of the Revolution. Now, while they wait to be able to say what they please, they have re-created and welded their forms, sensitive, new, to their liking. And, taking great risks, told marvelous tales. In their prose, they have reduced abundance to the one important indication. Their poetry is a mixture of the flesh, the tangible, and the revelation that mark the early days of all great periods.

The poet speaks as if he had just received the gift of sight. Cities and airports, trees and fields, and the long rivers that cut through them, are pressing against his talent. His meaning is revealed by the quickness of an image, the new placing and displacing of words. He knows no aloofness. From his finished poems comes a sort of wild blessing, even when for him, in spite of the snow outside, it is quite dark.

They are a nation of chess players. One has the feeling that at different times there was an interesting game to be played: staying alive.

It is curious that the government has not yet realized that the best export, the most shining, winning picture, is that of Russia in its fresh new talent (the freshest writers, not necessarily the young ones). The admiration of other countries goes not to what is said, but to the way it is said. Better one Joyce, better one Faulkner, than dulcet tones that leave no trace.

The reason Sinyavsky and Daniel could be given such severe punishment, out of proportion to the infringement of legality, is that the very thought of ridiculing your country abroad is unpopular. The artist is exceptionally privileged (physically) at home, and only a very, very small percentage considers him to be morally without obligations.

A man like Tvardovsky, who courageously publishes talented if unorthodox writers in *Novy Mir*, does more for the advancement of freedom than anything surreptitiously published abroad.

There seems to be a sort of murmur over their heads like the singsong of a Latin Mass in an Irish church, the high and low condemnations of capitalists and other sinners. No one pays much attention, and though eventually obedient to the priests, no one is much affected by this condemnation. Those most touched by it are the foreign correspondents. Impervious at first, after two years of reading the Russian press and listening to broadcasts, they begin to show in their texts a slow wearing out, a fatigue.

The Russian condition just now is that of ambiguity. They wish for liberty but are afraid of it. They wish for comfort but cannot face the disparity of rewards of a freer economy. They would like the world to be in their image, yet they know that the struggle for a fair livelihood is one thing, the struggle for the mind another. They hesitate.

During our stay, the times were known as those of the Yellow Light Period. Not yet green, but not still red. It had seemed a miracle that they be allowed to speak again. Though not too loudly. It is obvious that the economic evolution, or, rather, revolution, is of first importance. Why vilify the regime that is successfully trying to bring you this change for the better? If you upset the apple cart . . .

Shying Away

There is an aspect of Communism that is as obvious to them as it is to us: countries in the vanguard of literacy, well-being, and science do not need Communism. It is obvious, but they regret it. Because of a sort of indecency in capitalism—the

flaunting of wealth, the difference marked by wealth alone—
they shy away.

Philippe said: "They obviously no longer wish to be apart
from the world. *Ils veulent entrer dans la danse.*"

Later, before going to sleep, I kept thinking of the French
children's tune and its wise refrain:

> Come into the dance
> See how one dances
> Skip, then, and dance
> Kiss whom you please!*

Where do we differ? We too wish the most for man. But in
another way. It is perhaps that we secretly desire to be part of
an elite, a gifted group whose intelligence and imagination
will make us almost visibly different from others. Knowledge,
choice, will have us breathe a subtler air. In the same room with
others, we will know a more luminous climate. Aristocracy, said
the Greeks. The Happy Few, said Stendhal. But through some
force of simplicity, some sort of innocence in their nature, the
Happy Few have never interested the Russians. They take their
delight where they find it, spiritually especially, and are naturals
for global schemes about humanity.

Turning this huge mass of superstitious believers into anti-
God activists was not as difficult as it would seem. God had become "part of the great official lie," the better to hold the people
in ignorance and subjugation. Any self-respecting man must re-
alize that there was no God.

If one wished to rid oneself of misery, one had better rid oneself of the clergy along with other official outrages.

"There was no Fall of Man," said one of the proud early
deputies to the Duma. One gets today the feeling that they are
here to prove it.

* *Entrez dans la danse / Chantez, / Dansez, / Embrassez qui vous
voudrez.*

What we have and they have not as yet—cars, amusing gadgets, space to live in according to one's own rules of taste and not one's needs—one day they will have.

Liberty, tolerance, these are luxuries.

The Tretiakov

We stood in a room surrounded by huge icons, personages larger than life-size, draped in brilliant red over their coats of mail. Some in pink. Long, aloof, mysteriously strong. The saints were modeled after the princes of the time. Or the princes after the saints, though less likely. They have many more horses than our saints. They take them to Paradise, four and five at a time. The great Rublevs are also here.

Across the way, the house where Isadora Duncan lived with the poet Esenin. What were they like, the rooms where she danced so often late at night for their friends? She had left Paris for Esenin, but love could not help the young poet bent on destroying his talent. She returned to America and things got worse. Drink and rows. A calm period. Drink and rows.

One December in Leningrad, he hanged himself in a hotel room.

Ehrenburg quotes the lines Esenin wrote sometime, somewhere, not long before the end.

> Rustle, gillyflowers, mignonette,
> I would willingly drink in your company,
> Harm has come to my soul,
> My soul has come to harm,
> Rustle, July flowers.

One afternoon, in Paris, I went to an exhibition entitled "Under the Sign of Isadora."

It was in the small Bourdelle Museum, in the house Bourdelle the sculptor built for himself, with three studios, and two small gardens that seemed to come into and through the house because of open walks roofed over along the upper stories, half inside, half out. It was late spring and the trees were pressing against the house. There was no one else there that afternoon but two or three quiet, fascinated Asians.

Quantities of drawings of Isadora lined the walls, even the corridors, by Dunoyer de Segonzac, Maurice Denis, Gordon Craig. There were vivid small terra cottas by Rodin, his shrimp-pink water colors of her in the nude, Bourdelle's fascinating, beautiful drawings, and a few photographs and letters.

I went for a twofold reason. Because I had so often looked up at the window of the apartment in Moscow, thought of the stranger, this woman, surrounded by Russians of the Revolution, married to one of its poets. Soviet Russia was in the stage of the hardest poverty, and the greatest hope. The civil war and the war against the Allies had been won, Lenin was alive, and the artists were free. Isadora was herself a revolutionary, a reinventor of forms, from the time she danced in the streets of San Francisco as a little girl of six for her friends the street urchins. When eight years old, she was earning a little money.

I went also to see if I could understand something about her radiance, about her strength.

A figure, almost Victorian, curve leading to curve, except for a sudden strength and length of hands. The Victorian aspect is deceptive. The curve is only the outer line of the sleekly muscled body. She is more like the Kore, the young women standing in their bright-red room in the Athens museum, bold and strong and absolutely rounded. That is why she, Isadora, appealed so much to sculptors: the beautiful weight within the skin.

There is great beauty in this exuberant plumpness, a plumpness not of satiation, but of power. We, with our rage for thinness, seem to have forgotten it.

There were moments when an audience could not see her walk across the stage without rising from their seats. Why?

The means at her disposal—technique, cultural knowledge of the dance—were not very great. She drew from within herself, evidently in a state of divination, and danced her visions. Like every great artist, she at once had recognized exactly what she needed, and found her source of material in the scenes on Greek vases. She remembered the gestures of the Greek maenads, bacchantes, priestesses, with an astonishing precision.

"An almost imperceptible movement of her hand would be followed with emotion," said Segonzac. Emotion. That is what she shared with the audience.

Occasionally the long hands shut as if to claw, but no, surely she must have opened them soon again, and closed them rarely for more than the minute necessary to the shutting of the hand in coitus. She was not a holder; not a holder, she ran, and looked back. In a small terra-cotta model by Bourdelle the body is crouching on one leg, the other stretched backwards horizontally, the hands seeking the retreating air.

Rodin's drawings show extraordinary movement of a sort of violent purity, naked, yet with the noble sensuality of the young. The very early Greeks tried to give this suggestion of the sacred and the profane within the same being. You meet instantly, in Rodin's small clay models, the sculptor's surprise at her power. "Isadora Duncan takes from nature that strength which is not talent but genius." Thus Auguste Rodin.

In Bourdelle's drawings there is a frenzy of immediacy, the desire to seize the form for himself or for all time, before it changes.

Bourdelle was peevishly described by his contemporaries as being archaic, a belittling term in those days. He defended himself in words that bring him close to us and link him to Isadora's art: "They say this to punish me. The archaic is not naïve. The archaic is not poor. It is of a nudity so proud that those who cannot understand it find it poor, because it holds itself at a distance."

Her Paris friends watched over her. And what friends.

Elie Faure, the great art critic, Paul Poiret, who led Paris fashion by the nose, Mounet-Sully, the tragic actor, Nijinsky, Rodin, all loved her, wrote to her, waited about. Watched her. The eyes without make-up, eye shadow on the eyelid and underneath the lower lashes. The nose a little turned up, the small mouth shyly opened. The throat with a slight goiter, like the icons of the warrior saints in the Tretiakov. Small-breasted, long and thick-legged, sculptural.

She had a daughter by Gordon Craig and a son by Paris Singer. In 1913, Deirdre was seven and Patrick five. She had married Gordon Craig, but did not marry Paris Singer, who loved her devotedly and certainly delightfully, his profile as beautiful as his first name demanded, and, behind his continued generosity, the Singer sewing machines.

Isadora's apartment was on the top floor of a house in Neuilly, decorated by Paul Poiret.

Below the floor where she lived was a large practice room, with one wall of mirror, the others of pale pleated gray cloth. The children would sometimes ask their mother's accompanist to play for them. A visitor on his way to Isadora's apartment could see them running and leaping, their small arms raised in their mother's gestures, sprites hardly thicker than the air.

One night, in April, 1913, she danced at the end of her performance what she called the "Pleasure of the Moment." The audience went into a frenzy of clapping, even with the curtain down, the lights out, stubbornly refusing to leave. But she would not have supper after her triumph, and, feeling depressed, asked to be taken home.

The next day, both her children were drowned with their nurse, trapped in a car that glided into the Seine. The car had stalled, the chauffeur had got out to crank it, the car slid into the water. It was a long and useless rescue.

Bourdelle, a passionate admirer of her dancing (he would cut, into the very edges of his clay studies of her, words such as "Isadora," "Hymn Beyond Voice," "Forms Beyond Song"), had been in the audience the night before. "It is terrible, terrible," he said. "She is dancing Death." (He was given to extraordinary presentiments.) When leaving the theater, Bourdelle pointed to a car and said, "My God, how terrible, it's a coffin." Someone called from the theater entrance to ask for Mrs. Duncan's car. Then, the car that Bourdelle had seen drew up.

Isadora left for Corfu, moaning her pain in short letters to her friends. Yet even through these you feel the marvelously energetic body unable to keep from surging back toward life.

It was after the war that she met and married Esenin.

In 1925, Esenin is dead. In 1927, the red scarf around her throat caught in the wheel of her car and strangled her.

"No, I will not hold up the sky with my two arms," said Sappho one day in Greece, in 600 B.C.

"This is a copy." But of what? Of whom? There is a strange feeling that you sometimes get when you look at someone, knowing that they are an imitation, not necessarily unpleasant, but one you cannot trace, not having seen the original. In the little museum, lying in a glass case, was a photograph which took me straight into a winter of my childhood. I had been put, though only twelve years old, in a finishing school outside

Paris. It had been a mistake. The other pupils, a mixture of Rumanians, Poles, English, and a few stray Americans, were between sixteen and twenty years of age. My father had liked the shape of the house. It did not much matter. I had a lovely time for two terms, being taken constantly to the theater, when what I needed was some strong grounding in mathematics and more Latin. We would disguise ourselves once a week for dinner, to learn the ways of the world, the headmistress said. She would show herself to us before going off to her visits in Paris—to teach us how a Frenchwoman wore her clothes. Children are sensitive to people who pretend. Nothing seemed to me very natural in this school, but realizing that the outer world was probably very unnatural, I did not worry about it. Except that the headmistress remained in my mind as the image of someone I was in fact not seeing.

There, in a photograph of Isadora lecturing, I recognized the felt hat turned up on one side, the long scarf tightened around the throat, the musketeer wide-cuffed gloves negligently held. There was the image of the headmistress. This same plumage became the dress of many women, and the fashion continued for years.

Many a modest wearer had no idea that she had borrowed the feathers of such a shining and unconventional bird.

The Cloakroom

The new theater in Moscow seats three thousand people. The cloakroom is as large as the orchestra, of necessity, because you take off the contents of a wardrobe trunk before you sit down. After the performance hundreds are roped off to let other hundreds get their fur hats, boots, and coats, served up with lightning rapidity.

The Puppet Show for grownups is very popular and always packed. The success lies in having the voices of two excellent live actors accompany the puppets. The dialogue tells of foolish dreams, imperishable idiosyncrasies, and, sometimes, the new way the wind blows. A scene out of doors: children are playing ring-around-the-rosy, except for one, who stands apart, angry, near his grandmother. Two women come in and chatter about the ways of bringing up children: in kindergartens, with expert child care, very good; leaving them with grandmother, very bad. The New Way turns to the child: "You must join the others." Up pipes the smallest and youngest of voices in the world. "I will *not* be part of a collectivized society." Blackout.

"Why," said Vassi Katanian, "I had a copy of *Life* magazine. It showed a map of destructive weapons, missiles, all aimed in one direction. What are we to think? Who are they aimed at?"

"They are aimed at you, of course. Because you are very strong and very frightening. But Americans do not want war."

"Then why such articles in magazines?"

"To scare you, perhaps. Or to cheer ourselves up when we are a little downcast over our popularity."

They lost twenty million men in the war. Our figures give eighteen million for the Russian losses, but they count, I believe, the after-effects. They fear the Germans. They cannot forgive them, though they might do so in words. They will never again let their security be endangered where Germany is concerned. They are firmly convinced that the country could not withstand a second bloodletting on such an apocalyptic scale.

The heavy smell of the old brewery fills the street as it did in Tolstoy's days. His brown wood house, the orchard behind it, the courtyard, take up quite a bit of the street. The cloakroom is against the huge porcelain stove, so the coats will be warm when put on again. When you first go into the Tolstoy bedroom you wonder whether it is a passage or a small makeshift sitting room. Then you see a screen, and, behind the screen, two narrow beds of unequal length. The room is barely large enough to leave a passage on either side, to a door and to the vestige of a dressing table with celluloid combs. The pillows have wide, ruffled, linen pillow covers, used in Russia instead of pillowcases. There is no distance, nor air, between the beds. On the contrary, they look fastened together.

One remembers Tolstoy's descriptions of marital relationships, desire, surfeit, the nerves worn out in spent bodies, the rows, the distaste followed by hatred. He would flee sometimes and sleep on the leather couch of his study. But always returned. His conclusions and condemnation of what he called this destructive process were given in *The Kreutzer Sonata*. When his readers were advised to give up physical relationships altogether, many were puzzled. Hundreds of letters asked, if abstinence was really necessary, what would happen to the human race.

A few buckets of water would be thrown into the courtyard, it would freeze over, and there the family would skate. Tolstoy liked this especially. A photograph shows him from the waist up, towering above the wooden fence that separates the courtyard from the street, his beard floating in the wind, resembling a boat moving across a stage in front of the not-quite-believing spectators.

At arm's length, in the porter's lodge which they had made into a private printing press, he could see his wife, surely ignored by the Skater as he circled past. She was printing on the little hand press the first edition of *The Kreutzer Sonata*.

Rarer than Blondness

The white-faced, dark Russians have a romantic sort of beauty. The most fashionable women in Moscow, in handsome fur coats, are dark-haired. All of Tolstoy's heroines are dark.

Perhaps in reaction to the general, and to us rarer, blondness of the North.

The Kremlin Treasure

Friday was closing day, and because of the tremendous holiday crowds, we asked to go then.

The treasure is disposed in wide, high vitrines shaped like obelisks. All was dark. The guards were few and looked asleep. The light would fall on the obelisks from very high, one at a time, as we moved. Sometimes one, sometimes two would stay lit far back of us, taking on vague shapes of ships. The walls of the obelisks piled high with gold and silver would suddenly appear and black out. In the distance something white, a shell mounted as a bird, and something huge, a silver eagle. Nearer, as if coming toward us, an anthropomorphic shell, straight out of some story of a metamorphosis, the shell closely imitating a man's face, mounted in a swirl of gilt by a craftsman of Augsburg. Beautiful drinking cups on stems that must feel like silk in the hands, made of amber mixed with ivory. Then, some huge silver containers for wine, their tops unscrewing like milk cans a yard high. Close to the eagle sent by Christian IV of Denmark, a silver rooster, more the size of some Thanksgiving turkey.

The collection of English silver perhaps not as good as it is supposed to be. The Danzig pieces are superb, made for giants, of breath-taking beauty and splendor and haunting design.

Elizabeth I and James I sent some silver gilt cups to Ivan the Terrible and Boris Godunov. The Tsar Ivan asked for the Queen's hand, and was refused. He then offered her asylum should her subjects turn against her. The Queen was displeased.

Downstairs, with the carriages, the little blanket for Catherine the Great's horse, made of yellow feathers.

The crowns are all edged in fur, to keep the imperial foreheads warm in the bitter cold of winter apparitions.

The Zoological Garden

I sometimes wondered what we looked like to the Russians. Philippe all in dark brown, a brown sealskin collar on his long fur-lined overcoat, his *shapka* with its fur ears flapping in the approved manner as he walked down the street. "Man was once a Garden in a Paradise," wrote George Herbert. He would have felt surprise and perhaps pleasure at encountering me, a walking zoo. *"Elle portait sur elle un jardin zoologique,"* commented a Russian friend. The zoological garden consisted of a coat of snow panther, a bonnet of martens shaped like a ski helmet, boots of gray otter, a cream-color sealskin jerkin. Sheep had contributed several layers of woolen underwear. We had been warned to wear two pairs of gloves, the first of silk, the second of leather lined with wool or fur. I was never without a huge muff of blue fox, to carry indoor black flat pumps with black bows, the 1905 Baedeker, notebooks.

Leningrad

A marvelous-looking young woman, with reddish hair, quite a bit of eye make-up and red lipstick, was holding at arm's length her strong baby. She and the priest were in the act of immersing him several times, and the child was howling accordingly. At the other end, coffins, opened at the place of the head, the profile of the dead raised against the light.

"Philippe, you cannot take part in the baptism rites and also join the mourners. Especially the mourners."

"Why not?" asked Philippe. "They don't mind."

They didn't.

St. Isaac's

Leningrad is the only city to have a cathedral that changes the color of its skin. According to the winter weather, St. Isaac's turns from the red of its granite to a dark gray when it is only damp, then to a lighter and lighter gray as it gets colder, and when it snows, or is very cold, to bright white.

A leftover column, unused by the builders, was placed by Emperor Nicholas in the middle of the circle behind the Winter Palace. It turned white the day before we left and became unearthly against the pale yellow of the tsarist Officers School on one side and the green palace on the other. Though no Russian would allow it ever to be removed, it is, on its dark-red days, a flaw in such beauty. Perhaps the flaw without which there is no salvation, according to Henry James.

The Siege

During the siege of World War II, the people who lived on the top floors died first. They no longer had the strength to go up and down. It was a very cold winter, and the doctors counseled people to live together in one room of the apartment if they wished to survive, each one giving out some heat to the others. At first, the dead were taken down into the courtyard to be fetched by the city trucks. Later, people became too weak to carry the corpses down and they simply dragged them to some unused room at the end of a corridor and left them there. The windowpanes had been broken by the bombardments, and the windows were boarded up.

Our friend was only sixteen or seventeen at the time of the siege. She and her mother survived because the mother stayed much of the time in bed near the small stove that had been rigged up for them by a man in exchange for a gold watch and a ring. She would wait in line two to three days for a distribution of bread. People would replace each other so as to warm themselves before returning to the line. The friendships made while waiting in those lines still last.

The women in the factories stayed at their benches, too tired and weak from underfeeding to go home at night, afraid they would not get back.

Scarcity of Dogs

Dogs seem very few. Someone told us they had been eaten during the siege. But as early as 1865, Théophile Gautier remarked on the scarcity of dogs in Petrograd.

Saleswomen

All over the world, alas, most saleswomen in big popular-price stores are disagreeable. In Russia, a sort of aloof grandeur is added to this. They are functionaries of their government, and what are you? It is a little like going to the Pentagon for one's hairpins. One would expect them to look surprised, but not pleased. So it is with the Soviet saleswoman, sacred member of the State, keeper of the missing article.

Miod

Philippe went out to buy some honey. The word for honey is *miod,* and he was told to go to a store on the Nevsky Prospekt. When Philippe entered the store he was shown to a waiting queue. This let to the counter where he would find honey. Once in front of the saleswoman, after having been shown the *miod,* he was given a small ticket on which was inscribed a word and a price. He was then motioned over to some women customers whose practices he was to imitate. They went, ticket in hand, to another queue. When this queue arrived at its destination, he found himself looking up at a woman sitting very high above his head, a little like a referee at a tennis match. Philippe stretched his arm up to give his ticket, he paid, the woman rattled on her abacus, he received his ticket back, with another scribble on it. He then returned to the first counter. He took his place again in the first queue, much lengthened, but with new faces. He was then given the jar, waited a little, while it was wrapped up, and triumphantly bore it away.

These are the customary four stages to be lived through when purchasing anything in a sizable Soviet store. The Discovery, the Retreat, the Return, the Bearing-away. Such methods should be given much consideration when a country wants to put its economy "in reverse." To hamper and discourage purchasers.

The Young and the Old

There is a color cleavage between two generations. The older women wear putty-colored clothes, identical in tone, and no make-up. The young women make up their eyes in the early morning, wear brilliant kerchiefs or plaids over their heads, and colored dresses under their coats, which sometimes are made of an amusing imitation fur.

Fur Money

Squirrels' ears, and those of other fur-bearing animals, were used as money as late as the seventeenth century. The value of the currency was pegged to the value of the fur. The small ears of sable or ermine were of course of far greater worth than the red or gray squirrels'.

I like to think of walking up to a counter and exchanging many ears for one sable muzzle, which one could occasionally touch before spending it.

"There are so many animals on earth because they see God in so many different ways," writes Khlebnikov, and adds that in a very old Russian story, *The Tale of Igor*, it is said that "in animals perished many marvelous possibilities."

Khlebnikov's father was a scholarly ornithologist of great repute. The young writer took his exams in physics and mathematics, then studied natural history, then Sanskrit. Then and finally, literature, and writing.

Khlebnikov wandered about, poor, unable to settle, holding within his mind one of the most beautiful strange worlds in literature. He died half ill, half destitute, incapable of finding the practical strength it took to survive in Russia at the time, the man who had said, "Every man, in any city, should have a room to call his own."

This morning, the light has changed. The colored walls resemble the plumage of baroque birds, whose bright feathers glisten against the snow.

In front of great beauty, or great kindness in the sense of love, there is the "suspension of disbelief." This Coleridge knew and called it that. Better still, what Natasha Spender, the wife of the poet Stephen, said about André Malraux: "He delivers you from disenchantment." A walk in the sun, on a winter morning near the Neva, does that.

The Painters

We drove by some large buildings, well placed, their windows larger than other windows. "These are new studios for painters." "Will the painters be able to afford living in them?" "Yes." "Can they support themselves by their work?" "I know many who do," answered the well-informed friend. Some artists might prefer less conspicuous addresses.

These new apartments, this tender care, seemed to show a fear of the artist in line with Plato's. The artist is a disturber of public peace. The Russians' answer is efficient: do not outlaw the artist; keep him, hold him, pamper him. Let the State be to him a large soft body, and in his sleep, the body will roll over, and smother him to death.

Country Residences

The two imperial country houses are near Leningrad: Pushkin (Tsarskoye Selo) and Pavlosk. While the two great private houses, the Sheremetevs' Ostankino and the Yussupoff country place, Arkhangelsk, are both near Moscow.

Tsarskoye Selo and Pavlosk

There were evidently no limits to luxury, and, above all, no limits to distinction.

Distinction was a sensitivity. You could cover your walls, as Catherine did in Tsarskoye Selo, with amber or lapis lazuli, but you had to see to it that none of it overweighed, that there was not too much amber, too much gold, too much lapis. Your house helped you escape from a world of snow into one a little less shimmering than the gold, blue, and white outside. In summer, the soft greens of the countryside were prolonged into rooms such as the extraordinary green room at Pavlosk, with an arched Palladian ceiling, and endless windows, their shirred taffeta curtains just a shade sharper green. Next to the clover greens, pale-lilac rooms the color of the summer evening night.

The Russian temperament likes things on a large scale, but the other side of this temperament is a restraint, a reserve, when it comes to the splurge within. Not costliness for costliness' sake, but, rather, captive gaiety, the poetic mood, the remarkable workmanship, of which they are very proud. From 1812 to 1900, they built endless columned and porticoed houses resembling those of Natchez, retaining the Pavlosk taste for pure outlines with insides of pale, varied colors.

One wonders about the relationship between Catherine the Great and her Scot architect, Cameron. Before Pavlosk, which was built between 1780 and 1796, he added a pavilion wing to Tsarskoye Selo, and designed there for her some of the most enchanting furniture, somewhat as if Marie Antoinette's cabinetmakers, Jacob and Senné, had worked for the Brighton Pavilion. In the quieter Scottish vein, there is an Adam dining room, white reliefs on a pale-green-and-mauve background, and Cameron's chairs, lilies of the valley forming the backs, painted white and emerald green.

We walked by the Taurida, a marble palace. Somewhat like the Grand Trianon gone gray, built by Catherine for the favorite, Potemkin. Catherine loved this huge man, gifted with the most eccentric and sharpest of brains.

In the early days of their relationship, he was a magician exercising his charm.

Later she gave him power unequaled. She had slowly made him into an extraordinary and trusted statesman.

Seemingly lazy, and yet always at work, brooding, scheming, learning by conversation, dressed one day and not for weeks afterwards, attentive to the information he received from every corner of the earth, being given huge sums by the Empress yet paying her debts behind her back, Prince Potemkin gave the impression, according to Baron Nolcken, the Swedish diplomat, "that he alone ruled this Empire."

Sometimes the Prince would stay for several days lying half-dressed on a couch. People asked, "What is the Prince doing?" "He is thinking," would come the reply.

He annexed the Crimea for Catherine. He changed the condition and military worth of the Russian soldier. He was a great builder, constructed admiralties wherever there was a sea, drew and began cities that are today among the most famous of the Crimea. He allowed escaped serfs to settle unmolested in the new Southern Provinces, thereby attracting daring and intelligent runaways who became colonizers.

Potemkin had a predilection for all the Asiatic races inhabiting what were then the wastelands of the empire. He surrounded himself with his country's Central Asians, taking pleasure in their exotic looks and their strange qualities. Tartars, Kalmucks, Mongols, to whom were added Georgians, Armenians, and some venturesome French.

To frequent him was considerably more of an honor than a rest.

From Potemkin's house in Finland, Harris, the English Ambassador, wrote home breathlessly: "His way of life is as singular as his character. His hours for eating and sleeping are uncertain, and we are frequently airing in the rain in an open carriage at midnight."

This is not very different from the approach to life of quite a few Soviet citizens of today, who live along these lines with no one commenting. This liberty of behavior under a hard government Maurice Baring has already noted. Delightful as this is to me (the only cross I have found difficult to bear are meals on time), yet, when it comes to meeting with visitors or with each other, Russians are very punctual.

(This same Sir James Harris tried, as English ambassador, to get Catherine to send the Russian fleet and some troops to America to quell the revolt of the Colonies.)

At a time when Versailles was the master of fashion, Potemkin was renowned among foreign envoys for his taste. Corberon, the French Ambassador, describes a party at another palace of Potemkin's, the Anitchkov, next to the Hermitage, where the Prince sometimes entertained friends. "The small private rooms are charming; another cabinet, where the Empress took supper, was furnished in the loveliest painted Chinese taffeta and arranged in such a way as to resemble a tent. Around the walls of the cabinet, which can hold at the most five or six persons, was a little sofa. I noticed a particularly beautiful crystal chandelier manufactured by Potemkin's own glass factory."

Another evening there was an exquisite sterlet soup all St. Petersburg talked about, served in a bathtub of massive silver.

Catherine decided that she would never have enough men of the quality she needed to run her new and outspreading Russia unless she formed women capable of bringing them up, mothers whose character and education would be equal to raising these new potentates. She created a school for girls which she installed in a Rastrelli blue-and-white convent at Smolny, especially built very near the capital. The morning we went to see it, the walls were the color of a blue-green sea, solid against the white weightless earth, snow piled against white pilasters, white doorways. Through the white net of the trees the blue seemed meant more for pleasure than for a young women's convent.

She sympathetically housed a smaller school in a house next to the palace at Tsarskoye Selo communicating through to her own quarters by a suspended corridor. Potemkin's nieces were most carefully brought up there. Before or after their brilliant marriages, they each in turn became his mistress.

His close relationship with the Empress lasted seventeen years, from 1774 to 1791, when he died of a fever, in a field, near one of the cities he had built.

Just after she received the news of his death Catherine wrote to the German writer Grimm, known to pass harsh judgments, but a confidant of the Empress, ". . . my almost idol, Prince Potemkin, died after a month's illness. He had rare understanding, was singularly notable. No man had ever such a gift of witticisms as he. He was full of knowledge, and his ideas were forever new. He was magnanimous."

But to Potemkin himself she once sent a little note: "Calmness is for you a state that your soul cannot bear."

It Stretches Itself

The eighteenth century stretches itself into the nineteenth, and shows what probably would have happened in Europe without the two Napoleons, Ludwig of Bavaria, Queen Victoria, and without, above all, the romanticism which seems to begin, one is sorry to say, with Marie-Antoinette's hamlet. Rich rustic.

Pavlosk

Pavlosk was built by Catherine for her son Paul, later Tsar Paul I, who had great taste in the decorative arts and an intense interest in soldiers' uniforms.

Once the Empress Maria Fedorovna was a widow—Paul having been murdered, to everyone's relief—she continued the decoration of Pavlosk. She wrote down so carefully in her diary every aspect of every room that the restorers simply followed the number of armchairs noted, or the place of the ivory desk, of the ornaments and Chinese porcelains.

The outside of Pavlosk is a little disappointing, but inside begins enchantment. The Louis XVI overdoors are overrun with carvings of flowers; there are cornices and moldings of roses and jasmine everywhere, and delicate silk embroideries of flowers on the furniture. There is a set of armchairs looking like swans floating. Their enormously elongated necks are made into arms. The lean swans' gold necks were executed by the French *maître* Grosset from the designs of the architect Voronikhin, who was once one of Prince Stroganov's serfs. The Prince freed Voronikhin so that he might study at the St. Petersburg Academy, which serfs could not enter.

Pavilions are scattered about in the park. Countess Tolstoy, walking there one day, met a man who impersonated nightingales for the imperial family. He was very disagreeable, said the Countess.

The Empress did not like to sleep in her bedroom, but haphazardly, in a favorite drawing room, or wherever the end of the evening found her, the scented water (a sleep inducer) at hand, someone quickly throwing on a sofa the cover of lightest down incased in white linen that replaces sheets in Russia.

Lazy Poet

Beds play little part in this country. There are no great beds, no Charles II heights carved and scrolled, no silver bed like Nell Gwyn's, with the King's face and the head of a hound, no Elizabethan wooden enclosures, no ostrich feathers as for the French court. Beds must have been considered extremely temporary and, in themselves, of little interest.

With two exceptions. An iron cot, once Lenin's. And in Goncharov, Oblomov's, who wasted his life in his, but that is a bed in literature, and another story.

A story that could not, we trust, be written today. The State discourages idleness. The poet Joseph Brodsky was sent to cool his heels because, runs the accusation, he was lazy and refused to earn his living. He was warned, but continued without employment.

The idea of being punished and sent to prison for not taking seriously the task of earning one's living and preferring to write poetry offers wonderful possibilities for dialogue. Brodsky read his poems at evening reunions. From the report of the Committee on Young Writers' Work, it is clear he is not a poet. This accusation and verdict accentuate the impression that the whole country is a gigantic boys' school, where no one, ever, comes of age.

Another poet is publicly taken to task in the press for using too complicated forms in his poetry. The censors are right. They watch. Within new forms hides the anarchy of desire, the spirit wishing to break through.

"It's a bore," said Philippe, "this not being able to gamble with your life."

Restorers

Pavlosk was gutted. The Soviets have accomplished in both Pushkin and Pavlosk the most enchanting and complete restorations, even to the decoration of rooms that had been planned in their day in detailed water colors, but never executed.

You run your hand over the carved paneling and say, "But this cannot be a copy," and they show you the eighteenth-century instruments they had to work with or had remade to work as before, two hundred years ago, so as to leave no trace of the war. The brilliant restorers, among the most gifted of their craft, with unlimited means at their disposal, have decidedly overlooked restoring the faces of the last generation of Romanovs. You do not see a portrait of them anywhere. Faceless, bodiless, erased.

The Clothes Exhibit in Pavlosk

I kept to myself unfashionable questions about this invisible family. Though I believe a Romanov came here, and was charmingly and kindly received. As a tourist.

In the small apartments upstairs in Pavlosk, an exhibition of clothes, mostly imperial, very personally and chronologically shown, with accessories and portraits of their owners.

Catherine the Great's discreet woolen dressing gown, of palest pink but as ample as an army cloak. Suddenly, in a small vitrine in a little room at the end, the late last Empress' handkerchiefs, her gloves. Gloves of Russian leather the color of light-brown tobacco with a small white edging. Of an elegance such as Hermès could not think of attaining.

"This is the first time these have been shown. I must bring my mother here," said our guide.

The Russians may well carry this inherent elegance, this unconscious refinement, into their new world.

When true luxury is opened to them, they will probably leap far ahead of others who have been working at luxury for quite some time.

Hosts

One day at Emerald Cunard's, in New York, an old lady, Emily Iznaga, who had many English and Russian connections, told the following story. She and her friend Marie Sherketiev were both very young women just before 1917. Marie Sherketiev had been asked to a small reception at the Palace in Petrograd. Her hosts were the Emperor and Empress. Back in England, staying with her friends, she told of the experiences of the reception, of its guests, their looks and brilliance, how they sat, what they were served, what they wore. "And the Emperor, the Empress, what were they like?" Marie Sherketiev held up the square of her white handkerchief in front of her face. "No faces. They seemed to have no faces. When I looked up from my curtsy, they had no faces, no faces at all."

A Correspondent

We discovered that there was an Englishwoman, an enthusiast about Russian country palaces, who was corresponding with the curator of Pavlosk. We would have liked to send her a post card telling her that she had found fellow madmen, but a name in English, even in hieroglyphics, took too long to look up, and we had to leave.

Lordliness

A country, they say, can perhaps best be judged by its children. Here they are, playing under the snow-iced trees, strong and fat-cheeked, bundled in little fur coats of black seal or, more frequently, rabbit, but so sharp against the snow, topped by the favored green or some other color wool scarf tied at the back. Their fathers pull them in their small sleds along the street, and they lie back, clear-skinned lords of all they survey. They are hoisted to the top of the toboggan slide, sled and all, and they flash down and spin again and again at the bottom without a trace of anxiety. Calm and collected, true kings.

Children are not given all their presents on Christmas day, but one present a day for fifteen days, hidden under the tree. There are some delightfully complicated and small mechanical toys, mostly animals, no bigger than the palm of one's hand.

One huge store in Moscow is entirely devoted to children's toys and clothes.

Morning Theater

I suppose that one of the secrets of a successful life is to be made to bear as a child much that you do not understand. In the winter mornings, at half past ten, one goes to the children's performances, not, as in my childhood, children's plays, but the great ballets and the great operas. In this manner we saw Pushkin's and Tchaikovsky's *Eugene Onegin* and *Pique Dame* in the Kirov, the pale-blue-and-silver theater, packed with children. Leningrad, the most elegant of all cities, has two or three blue-and-gold or blue-and-silver theaters, the colors of those of Versailles. There was a little girl with a thin face and a heavy plait wearing a winged apron which came beyond her ears. On her narrow chest was pinned a decoration. People fussed over her, and she looked superior and rather disagreeable. Perhaps a heroine of school studies.

Realism

The realism in the Russian theater is so strong that it gives you a feeling of unreality.

The flat surfaces become three-dimensional, the lighting disquietingly exact, the actor himself ages under the old man's make-up. And where are you? Forty years back. No, perhaps one hundred.

The result is pleasant but old-fashioned. Though at times marvelously suggestive. In Gorki's *The Barbarians* there is a dinner party in a garden, a remarkable, to us nostalgic, scene of rich, aimless, and irretrievable country life.

In this country, everything once stated can be justly contradicted. When we had begun to give up hope we saw, in a small theater in Moscow, the boldest direction, by Lubimov, of Brecht's *The Good Woman of Setzuan.* Something beyond compare, fresher than what the East Berlin Brechtians can do. The performance of the two ambling musicians compassionately and sarcastically fulfilling their roles, the four gods in green bowler hats, made you feel wildly alive, but also witty and kind. Can one ask for more?

A Change

Russians are a complicated people, unafraid of complications. A welcome change after the French, who insist on clarity till the thought dries up, and the Anglo-Saxons, who are afraid to split hairs.

Eye Make-up

It is extraordinary what eye make-up does for the young Russian face. Without it the girls would have unlit, uncharacterized faces. But it is sufficient to elongate the eyes, to vaguely darken the lids, and you have a bone structure. Laughing or sleepy, sometimes luminous, faces, gossiping.

The Emperor was surprised. There was no protocol for such an occasion. A young American sailor from upstate New York had come to Russia to see the Tsar for no other purpose than to bring him a gift. The audience had been requested by the American consul and had been granted. He would be received in St. Petersburg, in the Winter Palace.

The young sailor entered with an acorn in his hand. He said to the Tsar, "This acorn fell from a tree that stands by the house of George Washington. You're a great ruler and George Washington was a great ruler, and I thought you might like to plant the acorn with me by your palace."

The poet Robert Frost told this story in Russia, when he was sent there by John Kennedy.

How had the young sailor managed not to lose this acorn on the journey from Virginia to St. Petersburg? Had he told his captain his adventurous plan?

It was surely planted. An oak tree. The climate is too hard; it might not survive. So they may have put in a symbolical one and sent the acorn farther south, and planted it in some public square, perhaps near one of the huge provincial universities. Such as the one in Kiev, very proud, painted red. Somewhere in this Russia, the young sailor has his tree.

The leaves of oaks stay green longer than those of other trees. Almost as if they would turn into evergreens. The leaves become a bad-tempered, surly green; they shrivel tightly, and hang on to the tree sometimes until spring.

History is not always very punctual. This was in 1830. Had the boy come thirty-one years later he would have met the tsar who abolished serfdom, in 1861, the very year of the American Civil War.

☙❧

"Unlimited Autocrat" was the Emperor's title. After the 1906 revision of the fundamental laws of the Empire, he was still Autocrat, but no longer illimitable.

(The Shorter Oxford Dictionary defines an autocrat as a monarch of uncontrolled authority.)

Proverbs

The French Minister Louis Joxe was made ambassador to Russia. He presented his credentials to Khrushchev. The new Ambassador was a great amateur of proverbs, and hoped to collect quite a few in a country where they were so highly prized. He was taken aback, however, when Khrushchev greeted him with the following: "The mother-in-law is all the more suspicious of the daughter-in-law when she herself, long ago, has put horns on her husband's brow."

Another useful proverb, though one hopes no longer needed as advice: "Go under the table, and find your friends."

Joxe on conversation: "Conversation is a game. If you must explain the rules to someone, it is difficult play."

The Time-browned Man

There is in the Hermitage a body. One returns to see it, and then again to know why one returned. Usually there is nothing more unflattering to the spirit than to come across drearily preserved bodies. They were meant to confront another world, and should do so. But not this one.

It is in a glass case, the body of a man, stretched out long and narrow, naked, the legs slightly drawn up, as when a boy asleep dreams of running.

What startles you most is not that he should be lying there, in his time-browned skin. There is something else. A sort of proud indifference to immobility, as if he had stalked pleasure and movement and laughter so well that his body would never forget it.

Just below the heart, crossing the body like an S down to the loins, drawn with the speed of a whiplash, there is a scar. With careful stitching, even, calm, and close, such as any surgeon might envy. Through the scar was ripped out all that would turn this body to corruption. Ice, and cold for centuries, did the rest. The head is turned a little to the side and upwards, and shows the oriental slant of the eyes. He has the highly arched feet of a man who doesn't walk much, but rides, or dances.

The Masked Horses

In the next room his horses' masks were hung up, as in a horses' clothes room. The masks, which reached down to the horses' nostrils, were made of flat, colored feathers or fur, dyed blue. They were surmounted by high antlers carved out of wood, and covered with gold. Tufts of wool dyed blue or red were tied to the ends of the antlers. High up where the antlers met, a bird sat, of wood, colored, perhaps from the dye of added feathers now gone. How dumbfounded the enemy must have been when they lined up in the sun on the hard snow of a Siberian field.

In a glass case the most feminine of possessions: a small pair of women's boots, stiffened at the top with embroidery.

The soles of the feet were embroidered with long, darkly brilliant pyrite beads. When the wearer sat cross-legged, or moved to dance, the soles shone in the light of the fire.

These Altai men were great lovers of embroidery. Also of tattooing, which is somewhat the same thing. Their clothes were often made of sleek dyed furs, in checkered patterns, embroidered. Embroideries beaded and speckled and gold-threaded, as delicate and complicated as the Elizabethans'. The women wore small, very tight-fitting baby caps of net, evidently to hold their black hair down their backs, loose, or in a long plait.

All this was found in the Altai, part of the huge country of the Scythians, a mountain plateau of Siberian Mongolia. Thieves broke into a burial mound. Through the hole they left by, water poured in. A sudden cold, and the water froze. In the spring thaw the earth veiled over the opening; sometime between 500 and 600 B.C. The ice preserved colors, furs, embroideries, and flesh until, as one would take blocks of ice from a stone house, these objects were brought out. A small purse is made out of a guepard's head. It came a long way over the pass, from India, and, when found, it was filled with medicinal herbs.

"Here when the King dies . . . they take the King's corpse, and, having opened the belly, and cleaned out the inside, fill the cavity with a preparation of chopped cypress, frankincense, parsley seed, and anise seed, after which they sew up the opening, enclose the body in wax, and, placing it in a wagon, carry it about through all the different tribes." So Herodotus. They steamed themselves in felt tents, first covering their bodies with a paste that left their skins very white. The characteristics of his Scythians, their love of strong liquor and steam baths, their suspiciousness of foreign customs, have not very much changed. The Altai people are probably those whom he sees as having griffins to guard their gold. "They liked only gold, used neither silver nor brass." Leather cups for the poor. The Russian Scythian is still addicted to steam baths and too often to drunkenness, according to *Pravda*. The gold is guarded, but the griffons have left, or turned into curators.

The Scythian Who Preferred Other Customs

The closest illustration of Herodotus' chapter on the Russians is the case of Nureyev.

"To this day, if you ask the Scyths about Anacharsis, they pretend ignorance of him, because of his Grecian travels and adoption of the customs of foreigners."

Anacharsis was a Scythian personage, a man of great education, an ardent traveler, a perfect product for export. He succumbed to the attractions of Greek life and secretly adopted Greek religious practices.

On his return from one of his trips someone spied him dancing with a tambourine, in a wood in the part of the country between the Dnieper and a confluent, called Woodland, because "it is covered with all manner of different trees." He was dancing with a tambourine, sacred images sewn to his person, in the Greek fashion. The story was told to the Scythian King. In the same Woodland, Anacharsis was found pierced by an arrow. Some say the King's own arrow.

We thought it only polite in the very city of Nureyev's ballet company to mention the effect of his talent on audiences in London, where we had last seen him, his extraordinary manner of taking a bow. At the word "Nureyev" they would look blank. The next time we told the story backwards: the enthusiasm of English audiences for ballet, the number of curtain calls. Much interest. At the mention of Nureyev, blankness. As if we were speaking of something too distant to hear clearly.

When one of their own people leaves them, they do not consider him a traitor. Those who leave seldom rate this label.

Their own life is still hard, they are not out of their difficulties. They feel they have been left for something softer, easier. Cars, traveling. They would like these too, as who wouldn't? So they simply decide that leaving is a little shabby. And the very name fades and becomes unfamiliar. "Anacharsis . . ."

Voices near me in the street, like honey, some dark, some light. Of the two people speaking on my left, one has in his voice something held back, some promise of future enjoyment. No hurry. Don't hurry. Laugh a little with me. We are engaged in some great adventure. We know this. But why hurry? Stay.

Atheism

Philippe, who is always dinning into me the abuses of religion (obscurantism, brakes put on scientific discovery, furtherance of ignorance), was almost made into a believer by a visit to the Museum of Atheism.

After finding the museum discouragingly large, Philippe became rather severe. "You must be more careful in presenting scurrilous material," he said. "This is not a French print. In the first place, there was never an Inquisition in France, never a religious tribunal. Furthermore, getting a tricolor flag gave the French quite a lot of trouble. A Revolution and quite a bit more. No French printer will ever make a mistake as to which way the stripes run. As for this . . ."

Not the happiest day for a bosomy atheist.

The Last Visit

We paid a last visit to the Hermitage, straight to some special rooms.

Their faces are turned westward here so that they are proudest of their European art, but what lies downstairs in rooms little frequented is perhaps the most entrancing. Collections of Russian Central Asia: Turkmenistan, Tajikistan, Uzbekistan and those words Samarkand, Bokhara.

We found a woman guardian dressed in clothes usually associated with some unillustrious night-shift job. She turned out to be a great scholar, unassuming, comfortable, reassuring.

Behind locked doors easily opened, in a room like a safe, into which we slipped, silver of Tamerlane's that would have stilled Marlowe. And the delicate clothes of the conquerors, stenciled with designs of leaves and embroidered.

Statues of men, headless. When the heads exist they are as large as the body with caps like Rouault's clowns. They hug themselves with their narrow arms and hold against their chests a large quiet bird. The stone as if impregnated with sun.

Anna Akhmatova, the poetess, a great wounded feline who died last year, had spent some years in Russian Central Asia. She loved this Asiatic part of Russia: "Like drinking my own desires from someone else's hands."

The Apartment

The night before we left we gave a small dinner party in our apartment. The head waitress brought us some frail dark hyacinths, the very first. Just enough for a glass and a few on the tablecloth. Philippe and I will never forget those small fresh sprigs.

We loved that apartment. It was at the top of the Astoria, floating in sun. Philippe slept in the study off the sitting room, surrounded with birchwood seats, leather-cushioned. My room had been vaguely done in the modern manner and resembled a girl's room in a reformatory. In the center, a small but splendid drawing room. I wished we could take this apartment every winter of our lives.

What can one return for so much given? The snowflakes against one's face, the colors like a feast, the long love. There was a gift sent once, by Paul, long ago, the best of all. It came in the shape of a beloved friend: ". . . whom I have sent back to thee in his own person, that is, my very heart."

We walked for the last time to the Neva, invisible and covered in mists, then back by a short cut through the children's park. Children were playing in the half-light under the iced trees. I thought of the passage in *The Tale of Genji*, the little girls sweeping the snow with the tips of their long black hair as they run about.

Travelers bring home regret, a nostalgic desire, more or less effective, to return. With Russia it is total infidelity. You wish to go there, and never to come home. And you don't know quite why, which is the worst sort of infidelity, the kind that does not bear self-examination. You arrive in Denmark and sit for three days in Copenhagen. Everything seems easy. Your breakfast appears in ten minutes, everyone says, "Yes, right away, we will get it for you right away, anything you ask for."

Paris, May 9, 1966
Venice, May 6, 1967